In The King's Prison

In The King's Prison: A Journey of Divine Freedom

ISBN 978-0-9827710-7-5

Published by:
Noahs Ark Publishing Service
8549 Wilshire Blvd., Suite 1442
Beverly Hills, CA 90211
www.noahsarkpublishing.com

Edited by Elyse Wietstock
Cover Design by Theodore Wright IV
Interior Design by James Sparkman

In The King's Prison

A Journey of Divine Freedom

Fidel Donaldson

Noahs Ark Publishing Service
Beverly Hills, California

I dedicate this book to my mom, Mrs. Monica Maxwell.

You have always personified and exemplified discipline and tenacity. The sacrifices you made and the hardships and suffering you endured, both in Jamaica and when you emigrated to America to help your children, have motivated me to never give up in life.

My love for the outdoors came from the times you took me out to the backyard of our house in Queens. You taught me about planting callaloo, and the beauty of rhododendrons and azaleas. I am amazed by your versatility. You cooked and baked with the best of them, you are an excellent seamstress, a real estate investor; to sum it all up—you are the quintessential renaissance woman.

I love you Moomy.

Contents

Introduction

ON A FRIDAY NIGHT IN February 2020, my wife and I attended an inspiring gospel jazz concert. At its conclusion, the artist stood to thank the audience for attending and mentioned he owned a publishing company. My heart and soul were immediately stirred as I'd been diligently searching for someone to help me with my next publication. Already inspired by his great music, I knew he was the one! I had gone to the concert to enjoy a night out with my wife Paulette and walked away with a divine connection. This very creative mind would make my dream come true and my destiny a reality.

I was born into poverty in the violent inner city of Kingston, Jamaica. When I was five years old, my mother dutifully relocated to the United States in search of a better life for me and my siblings. After she left, I faced many hardships, including being molested by a female caretaker, unmercifully bullied by people of my own race, and chased and called the N-word by people I have never met. This fostered a lifestyle of crime and confusion.

How did I overcome it all? My experiences have compelled me to share my story with others. Being a native of Jamaica, growing up in New York City, and serving time in HMP Swaleside in England has given me a global mindset. Through all my life experiences I've discovered my true purpose and calling in life.

In The King's Prison is sure to inspire, motivate, and transform your life and empower you to transform the lives of others! Like the coronavirus pandemic, the increase of social injustice has infected our world. The bold initiatives introduced on these pages offer new solutions to an age-old problem. I am an advocate for the bullied, lost, and the hurting. Giving my life and voice for social and divine change is my charge!

CHAPTER 1

Road to the King

WHAT'S YOUR NAME?

Every human being is connected to an ancestral path, a journey, roads travelled by family members who lived before them. Many blacks in the diaspora have ancestral roots which can be traced through paths of slavery in America and the West Indies. Many of our ancestors came chained on different ships but wound up in the same proverbial boat. The paths our ancestors travelled, the journey they were forced to take has a great deal to do with how we think and live individually and corporately. The forcible removal from their homeland in chains and shackles, packed into unsanitary slave ships like sardines, where they had to defecate and urinate where they stood and sat would have been savage enough. The barbarism was exacerbated by the forced change of their names, as viciously depicted in Alex Haley's television miniseries *Roots*. The stripping of their culture forced our fore parents to adopt languages, dress codes, and ways of thinking that were different from their indigenous culture. The deep cuts on the back of the slave from the slave master's unrelenting whip would heal but the psychological scar would last for years. What would last for generations is the loss of identity.

One of the key identifying characteristics of a group of people is the common language they share. Listen to the black people in America and the West Indies and you will notice communication is done through languages not native to the continent of Africa. Listen to their names and the way they dress, and you will hear and see the influence of Europe, the ancestral home of the slave masters, though the people of the Caribbean have some traces of their connection to Africa. For generations black children in the diaspora were not allowed to assimilate into American and Western European society because they were told their black skin was a mark of inferiority.

In a conversation with my friend and mentor, Mr. Laval Belle, he told me that I was an advocate. I have a pretty good idea what the word means but I wanted an official definition, so I went to an online dictionary and found this definition: "a person who publicly supports or recommends a particular cause or policy." As far back as I can remember I always had a soft spot in my heart for the poor and underprivileged. When Mr. Belle called me "advocate," it gave me an understanding of the reason I joined a group called NYPIRG when I attended Queens College in New York. NYPIRG stands for New York Public Interest Research Group. It is a not-for-profit, student-directed organization that has existed since 1973. It was founded by Ralph Nader and Donald K. Ross as a public interest advocacy group. In retrospect, being an advocate is what led me to agree to march for a man who was going to be executed for a crime he did not commit.

I remember the day the white lady came knocking on our door in Corona, Queens. She told my mother about the injustice being perpetrated against a man wrongly accused and sentenced to death. There was a march planned and she wanted to know if we could support it. I had read stories of Dr. Martin Luther King, Jr. and the marches he led against inequality, but coming from Jamaica I was not accustomed to marching. In Jamaica many people protested inequality with bottles, knives, cutlasses (machetes), and guns. The idea of peaceful resistance and turning the other cheek was and is an alien concept to many Jamaicans.

It was a very cold winter day when the woman came. My mother told us, "If this white lady could come to our neighborhood on behalf of a black man who was going to be put to death, then we should go." I went with my sister Janet. None of our other siblings wanted to go because it was very cold. I was only a teenager then, but I had already experienced what it was like to be wrongly accused. I knew what it was like to be targeted because I was different. My desire to give my energy to a worthy cause trumped my desire to stay inside where it was warm. We marched for several hours in the freezing weather but at the end of it I felt a sense of accomplishment, a sense of purpose. There was a sense of empowerment. A multiethnic group coming together to advocate on the behalf of someone who was a victim.

When mentor Belle put a name to it for me, I became conscious of my true purpose in life. I lived advocacy but never thought about it as my purpose until I heard the word "advocate." Advocating on behalf of the less fortunate is not something I decided to do on a whim. It is in my genes, in my DNA. Who we are is largely determined by the DNA we received from our parents and our fore parents, but also greatly influenced by the society and culture in which we are raised.

I've never ascribed to the theory of nature versus nurture. I believe the sum total of who we are is an amalgamation of both. DNA determines who we are anatomically, how we physically look and sound, but environment plays a major role in how we think and act. The experiences I had as a child in an impoverished community in inner city Kingston, emigrating to another low-income community in New York, affected my outlook on the world, and affected the decisions I've made throughout my life, both for good and for bad. I was raised in homes whether led by both parents, my mom as a single parent, or my grandparents, where manners and discipline were instilled in me. We had to say good morning, good afternoon, and good night when we encountered an adult. If we acted up outside the home, adults in the community were allowed to discipline us which included a whipping if they deemed it necessary. They definitely believed in the words, "spare the rod, spoil the child." Some adults were diligent in their desire to make sure I was not spoiled. Getting an education was a must; being a dunce was not tolerated. As a child in school, time out was not a form of punishment when I acted up or did not do well on a test. Corporal punishment was the solution. Sometimes my wife and I are watching a movie and the child cusses out the parent, or sometimes we are in public and see a child screaming at their parent and throwing a fit and we smile to each other because we both know most Jamaican parents would not tolerate such public outbursts. The effectiveness of corporal punishment and whether it is right or wrong is something people will always debate. I'm writing about my reality, a cultural norm that I lived and experienced.

I feel compelled to look at both the nature and nurture side of the equation by learning as much as I can about my family history, at least the experiences and decisions of my parents and their parents before them. With DNA testing and the onset of companies that can trace a person's family history through these tests, it is a lot easier for individuals to know who their ancestors were. Prior to the breakthroughs in DNA research, people had to rely on oral and written history to know anything about their distant relatives —DNA can inform us about who we are related to biologically, but oral and written records let us know how our ancestors thought and lived.

Knowing that I am an advocate, I had a strong desire to find out which one of my parents I received my love of social advocacy from. I called my father and asked him a series of questions. The information he shared with me was very enlightening. I found out that both he and my mother were socially conscious; both of them advocated on behalf of the poor and needy. Both were part of an organization that advocated for better wages and living conditions for the poor.

JAMAICA—LAND OF WOOD AND WATER

The island country of Jamaica is the third largest island of the Greater Antilles and the Caribbean, after Cuba and Hispaniola. The indigenous people of Jamaica were Arawak and Taino. The Tainos called the island Xaymaca, which is from the Arawakan language; the word means, "Land of Wood and Water" or "The Land of Springs." When Christopher Columbus came with his men in 1494, many of the indigenous Arawaks and Tainos were either killed by the Spaniards or died of the diseases they brought to the island. African slaves were transplanted to the island for free labor with the approval of the Pope of Rome. In 1655 England conquered the island, renaming it Jamaica. When the British took over, Jamaica became a leading exporter of sugar. This plantation economy was dependent on the African slaves and their descendants. In 1838, the slaves in Jamaica were fully emancipated. The freed slaves chose to have subsistence farms rather than work on plantations, only growing enough food to meet their needs and the needs of their families. Even before this emancipation, slaves in Jamaica didn't simply accept their plight. The Baptist War, also known as the Sam Sharpe Rebellion, the Christmas Rebellion, or the Great Jamaican Slave Revolt, was an eleven-day rebellion that started on December 25th, 1831 and involved up to 60,000 of the 300,000 slaves in Jamaica. The uprising was led by a black Baptist preacher, Samuel Sharpe and waged largely by his followers. On August 6th, 1962 Jamaica gained independence after 300 years of British rule. Some may say it is coincidence, but I say it is divine intervention that I was born on July 22nd, 1962, the same year Jamaica received its independence from colonial rule. Born the year of Jamaican independence and given the name Fidel which means faithful, from the Latin word fidelis.

My dad Albert Donaldson was born in the Parish of St. Thomas on the Island to Eustace and Gladys Donaldson. "Mrs. Gladys," as my grandmother was affectionately known, had one daughter before she married "Uncle U," my grandfather. They had nine children together, though one unfortunately died at three years of age. Eustace's father was a Caucasian man from Scotland. Our last name

Donaldson is a Scottish name. His father objected to him marrying a black woman.

Like many other families who lived in the country in Jamaica, they had a lot of land on which they raised animals and planted and harvested crops. Eustace and Gladys Donaldson were both devout Seventh Day Adventists. Eustace was not only deeply spiritual, but also an intellectual who could converse with the brightest minds on geopolitical history. He had a heart to help people, so his politics were progressive. He was also exceptionally skilled at carpentry, a skill he taught my dad and his older brother Amos along with painting. He instilled in them a love for community, a desire to alleviate the suffering of the people around them however they could. My grandparents always cooked enough food so those in their community who were less fortunate could have something to eat. There was always a knock on their door by some neighbor who needed oil, sugar, or some flour.

BUSH DOCTOR

My grandfather was also a naturopath, a practitioner of holistic medicine. In Jamaica, a naturopathic person is called a bush doctor because of his or her knowledge of the medicinal uses for different herbs. It is a common practice for these individuals to go into the bush and return with herbs to make tea, cook with, and treat sicknesses. My grandfather knew different plants and roots which could be used for natural healing. I have strong memories of my grandfather boiling a tonic called wood root. I vividly remember him brewing and stirring the tonic in shiny kerosene pans. He was famous in the community for this tonic, which was made from Sarsaparilla, something called strongback, dogwood, chaney root, and a host of other natural herbs and roots.

There was an episode on the Dr. Oz show when he was told by a Jamaican lady in the audience about using strong black coffee mixed with Jamaican overproof rum to break a fever. Dr. Oz told her, "That is a myth." But it is not a myth to me. I remember the first time my sister-in-law Maureen suggested that remedy when I had a fever and flu-like symptoms. My wife boiled the coffee, put the Jamaican white rum in there, and told me to drink it while it was hot. It was rough going at first; the taste was strong, but I felt so terrible I had to do it. I covered myself after drinking it and several hours later my clothes were soaked with sweat and the fever was broken.

We have a fruit in Jamaica called Sour Sop. Jamaicans have used its leaves to boil tea for what we call 'donkey years,' in other words a very long time. Another name for Sour Sop is Graviola; if you google the word "graviola" you will see articles such as one on the Memorial Sloan Kettering Cancer Center website which had this to say about graviola: "Graviola showed anticancer effects in lab studies. Human data are lacking. Extracts of graviola have been shown to be effective against a number of viruses, bacteria, and parasites in test tubes. Laboratory studies have also shown graviola to be effective against some types of cancer cells. It contains chemicals called acetogenins, which are thought to be the active ingredient." I respect Dr. Oz, but no one can convince a Jamaican that home remedies are a myth.

HIM BAD LIKE YAWS

My father told me a story of a couple who lived next to them who quarreled constantly. One day my grandfather asked them why they argued so much. The wife responded in animated patois, "after him naw no use," meaning her husband was impotent and was no use in bed. My grandfather never encountered a problem in his community he did not try to solve and this one was no different; he had a remedy for what ailed the husband. There was no Viagra at the time. He boiled one of his concoctions known for helping impotent men and gave the man two bottles. Two weeks later he asked the couple why they were so happy, and the wife responded, "because him bad like yaws," meaning he was performing like a champion. Eustace had a medical book and knew all the organs in the body and their functions. There were times when he was able to tell a sick person there were impurities in their blood. He told others their sickness was from an improper diet. He was a true renaissance man who taught the people in the community not only the wisdom found in the scriptures, but also geography, history, and politics.

He was a fit healthy man with a razor-sharp mind. I remember how devastated I was when my dad told me he was hit by a car and killed. He was the first person I was very close to who died so it was very difficult to deal with. My dad told me something Uncle U told him, and it helped me tremendously in the grieving process. Uncle U told him, "In the midst of life we are in death." My dad was living in America at the time and attended the funeral in Jamaica. When the hearse brought the coffin from the church to the graveyard, six women carried it from the hearse to the burial site. My dad asked his brother Vincent who the women were, and Uncle Vincent smiled and said he would tell him later. Uncle Vincent later told him they were "the fish women." They bought fish and sold it in the market. When they had no money to buy fish, they could count on Uncle U to lend it to them. They wanted to show their love and respect by carrying his coffin. At the time of his death "the fish women," along with many others owed him money. My dad and his siblings forgave their debt because that is what he would have wanted them to do.

The family came from very humble beginnings in Jamaica, they lived in a small house made of bamboo, but the children were raised to love and revere God. They had to wake up at five every morning for prayer which would be led by grandfather Eustace. When parts of Jamaica were ravaged by a storm commonly referred to as the "Fifty-One Storm," many of the homes which were bigger and stronger fell, but my grandparents' bamboo house stood tall; a product of prayer and an unwavering trust in God.

I have no memory of my maternal grandfather Stafford Maxwell, he died before I was born. He was from the parish of Clarendon. My maternal grandmother Edith was a devout Christian who played the organ in the local church. She would eventually convert half of her house into a church. I remember her getting up early in the morning to sing "I Come to the Garden Alone." My mom and dad attended lectures at The University Of The West Indies and organized for the PNP, The People's National Party. When they felt the PNP was not doing enough to help the poor, they joined Marcus Garvey's movement. Garvey started the Universal Negro Improvement Association (UNIA), which was the largest mass movement in African American history. My mom was given the opportunity to visit Cuba after the revolution and when she was pregnant with me, she and my dad conferred with my grandfather Eustace and they decided to name me Fidel after the man who led the Cuban revolution. As a child I knew I was named after Fidel Castro, but through the conversation I had with my dad I learned a great deal about their progressive socialist beliefs. As a child I was teased when I told someone my first name because Fidel Castro was considered a pariah in America due to his ties to communist Russia.

CUBA LIBRE?

I am a staunch advocate of democratic principles, especially individuals having the right to vote for their leaders. I believe in a free market system where the playing field is leveled; an economic system free of nepotism, cronyism, and economic racism. What I have no problem criticizing vociferously is hypocrisy. I could never understand why China, a communist country, had favored trade status but Cuba was under a blockade. Yes, Havana is 105 miles from Key West and 228 miles from Miami; I get that America does not want a communist country on its border. But, if it was truly about democracy, then why was the blockade not in place under Fulgencio Batista the Cuban Strong Man? If you are truly against communism, then why are you willing to deal with one nation and not the other? Then I realized it was more about economics than politics.

Only the truth can make someone free, not political sound bites or "fake news." With that said, I present to you some background information on Fulgencio Batista. A Cuban laborer turned army secretary, Batista rose to power during the Revolt of the Sergeants in 1933. During this time, he appointed himself chief of Cuba's armed forces and controlled the five-member "pentarchy" that acted as the collective head of state after the overthrow of the Machado government. Batista remained in power via a string of puppet presidencies until he himself was elected president in 1940. At the end of his term in 1944, he left Cuba for Florida, returning to run for president again in 1952. When it was clear Batista was going to lose the election, he led a coup against President Carlos Prío Socarrás and seized power with the support of the United States government. Once in power again, Batista suspended his 1940 Constitution and revoked many political liberties, including the right to strike. Under the Batista dictatorship, the wealth gap between rich and poor Cubans widened as he allied with wealthy landowners to exploit Cuba's sugar industry and other commercial interests for the benefit of mostly U.S. companies. In response to growing discontent among the Cuban people, Batista tightened media censorship and attempted to repress demonstrations with widespread violence and brutality. It was in this environment that Fidel Castro rose in popularity and influence.

When it was clear Batista would be ousted, the United States withdrew their support of his government and waited to see who would emerge victorious after the revolution. Fidel Castro was sworn in as Prime Minister, but the U.S. government would famously come to oppose him when it was obvious he would not be as deferential and cooperative as Batista. Castro went on a "charm offensive" trip to the United States in 1959, but it was largely unsuccessful with government officials. Before leaving for Cuba, Castro met with Vice President Richard Nixon, having been deliberately avoided by President Eisenhower. Nixon had hoped he could temper Castro's radical views, but concluded that he was "either incredibly naive about communism or under communist discipline—my guess is the former."[1] I'm sure Castro was not naive about communism, but that he saw the effects of American Capitalism when it backed the puppet Fulgencio Batista.

We need the truth, the whole truth and nothing but the truth. When the racist white apartheid ruling class in South Africa attempted to overrun Namibia, Cuban troops fought alongside other soldiers to repel them. I may not be a communist, but I am proud to be named after any revolutionary willing to stand up to colonial expansionist bullies. Every group of people should have the right to self-determination. Whether they are Israelis or Palestinians, whether they are from England or Northern Ireland. Patrick Henry's famous words, "give me liberty or give me death" should not only apply to white colonists in the Americas seeking independence from the King of England; it applies to all people, irrespective or color or creed.

FRIENDS IN HIGH PLACES

My dad and his older brother Amos worked tirelessly on behalf of people who were unemployed and underemployed. There was a government-run employment center where my dad, uncle and other men went to seek work. During the tenure of the JLP, the Jamaican Labor Party, the Minister of Works was The Honorable Cleve Lewis. When one party was in power, they gave contracts to the people of their own party. Since my dad and his brother were active in the PNP, the chances for a contract were very slim. However, my mom's sister was very close to Mr. Lewis and his family, and she spoke to the minister who put my dad and his brother's name on the list to get a public works contract. When their names were added to the list, my dad and uncle Amos did not forget the men who were less fortunate. They continued to stand in line with them, encouraging and educating them. One day Mr. Lewis asked his secretary to ask my dad why he was still in line with the other men when his name was on the list to receive a contract. My dad told her, "God called me to lead those men," to which she responded, "Say no more Mr. Donaldson, that is well spoken." My family's roots of giving back to the community run very deep and that is why the lifestyle I would eventually choose was shocking to many, including myself.

MOM-SENSE

My mother was and is a feisty, hard-working, and intelligent woman. Today she is in her eighties and lives in her own apartment, still drives, and does a lot of work even though she is on dialysis. Prior to emigrating to the US, her dad planned for her to study in England but turned against her when she became pregnant. She also had an aunt on her mom's side who was living in the US who rescinded an offer for her to come and live with her. This aunt sent her thirteen pounds to help with travel expenses, but when she found out about the pregnancy she wrote my mother a very nasty letter telling her she was like a pig in a sty. The rejection by her father and the insult from her aunt caused a deep scar in my mom which affected her for years.

Someone in the community had a shop selling men and women's undergarments and accessories that was going out of business, so my mom took it over. The business thrived, so she bought herself a sewing machine and started a dress-making business. She learned to be a seamstress from her mom. My mom was a fighter with an entrepreneurial spirit who refused to let anyone hold her down. At that time businesses had to be closed on Sundays. My dad told me a story of one particular Sunday when my mom was in the shop and a policeman came in and threatened to prosecute her for being open on Sunday. As my dad was about to speak on her behalf to the officer, my mom beckoned him to wait, then proceeded to tell the policeman that there were many people committing serious criminal offenses and he should be out investigating them. She told him to get out of her store and dropped a name on him of someone in government who was high up; she threatened to report him if he did not leave her shop, which he did.

My mom was never one to back down from a challenge. She came from a line of people who fought for change. Her mother Edith Maxwell, née Peart, was related to Marcus Garvey's niece. Mr. Garvey's niece was a regular visitor to my grandmother's home. Both of my maternal grandparents used to attend the UNIA meeting that was held at a place called Liberty Hall on King Street in Kingston. In those meetings they heard the fiery speeches of The Honorable Mr. Marcus Mosiah Garvey.

As previously mentioned, the Universal Negro Improvement Association was founded by Marcus Garvey, a Jamaican immigrant to the United States. The UNIA was a Pan-African organization which came to prominence in the 1920s. After Garvey's deportation to Jamaica in 1927, the group's prestige and influence declined, but it nonetheless had an effect on African-American history. The UNIA was said to be the most influential anticolonial organization in Jamaica for its time, founded to work for the advancement of people of African ancestry around the world.

Liberty Hall was later used by Mr. Chris Lawrence. When he took it over, trade unionists from across the island came there to meet and strengthen their cause. One day, Mr. Lawrence told the audience that my dad would chair the meeting because he was very knowledgeable on parliamentary procedures. My dad worked tirelessly to educate himself in order to be more effective in what he considered his divine calling, the uplifting of the underclass. He attended lectures in a place called Almond Town, where a brilliant Jewish attorney held lectures on subjects like European history and socialism. The terms "progressive" and "socialism" have been in the media a great deal as we approach another presidential election. When I hear those words, I think of my mom and dad, two pioneers who worked hard to help people of all walks of life make social and economic progress.

Strong social advocacy roots were in my parents' DNA and the apple didn't fall far from the tree. In Jamaica we also say, "what drops off the head drops on the shoulder." Although he was an advocate, my dad was mild mannered and easy-going. My mom was a woman of action who had no problem telling someone what she thought. She was a fearless proponent of justice for the people. She visited Cuba at a time when there was a travel ban in place. Her passport was seized upon her return to Jamaica, but she had friends in high places and had no problem getting it back. While my dad and his brother were traveling throughout the island advocating for social change and a more just society, my mom ran her business until she had the opportunity to get permanent residence in America. Her aunt, Teacher Barnes, a highly educated woman who spoke perfect English was asked by her husband to relocate to be with him in Liberia along with their children and my mom. Teacher Barnes told her husband that she did not want to move to Liberia. She loved teaching children and was a very successful woman in Jamaica. If things had turned out differently, I might have been born in Liberia.

Teacher Barnes had contacts in the Jamaican government and was able to set up an appointment for my mom to apply for a visa to visit America. At that time in America there was not as much hostility towards people from economically underdeveloped countries who were seeking a better life. Teacher Barnes' contact must have been very good because instead of a temporary visa to visit America, my mom was given permanent status. It was a time of celebration for my parents; the opportunity to live and work in America meant a chance to help their children get a better education. My mom would take full advantage of the American Dream although she also experienced some nightmares in doing so.

As great as the opportunity was for my mom, and as great as it would be for all her children, the visa was a double-edged sword. Obtaining permanent resident status in another country meant my mom would have to leave her children. We had loving grandparents, but Mom is Mom and no one can replace her. My mother's relocation to America was for a noble purpose but left me feeling abandoned and set the stage for my journey to The King's Prison, a journey which would become the catalyst for my Divine Freedom.

CHAPTER 2

Abandoned

I WAS FIVE YEARS OLD when my mom left Jamaica to live and work in America. People who visit tourist areas in Jamaica like the beautiful Dunn's River Falls in Ocho Rios probably wonder why any native of Jamaica would leave such a beautiful island to live in another country. Vacationers visit places which are like a piece of paradise; they are not exposed to the blight, the systemic poverty which breeds violence in certain communities on the island. I remember the first time one of my daughters visited the north coast and stayed in an all-inclusive hotel. She dined on delicious Jamaican food, walked and swam in the pristine beaches; when she came home, she phoned me and told me she was moving to Jamaica. I told her there is a big difference between vacationing in a ritzy place and living in the area where the vacation spot is located.

There was a television show way back when hosted by Robin Leach called, *Lifestyles Of The Rich And Famous*. The show displayed the ostentatious, opulent lifestyle lived by rich and famous people. It is only a very small percentage of the world's population who are able to live this lifestyle. I thank God for the opportunity to live in America because the average household income here is higher than most other countries. A political science professor once told our class, "being poor in America is not like being poor in other countries." With that being said, my mom always told me, "don't forget where you came from." When you remember your struggles, you will have a greater appreciation when you are freed from them.

THE OUTHOUSE

I will never forget the house without an indoor toilet or electricity, the burning of a kerosene lamp to illuminate the room, Granny cooking on the makeshift stove using wood. I remember the large drums placed in the yard to catch water when it rained. I remember people carrying water in containers on their heads when rainfall was scarce. I remember the pants with holes in them, walking and running bare feet in the lane. I remember the rocks, bottles, and the occasional sound of gunfire which always erupted in an election season. Jamaicans willing to kill and maim each other for the meager resources the winning government would dole out to them, or simply because one said PNP and the other said Labor. There are some things experienced in life which become etched in our subconscious mind. I remember walking with my sister in Kingston one night and violence erupted in the streets. We had to dodge rocks, bottles, and all kinds of projectiles being hurled through the air. No one should be subjected to an environment like that, especially a child. The wealthy nations of the world could wipe out poverty if they had the will and the desire to do so; they could make sure every child gets basic medical care if they wanted to, but some countries love the status quo because they can exploit the poor for their own benefit. Unlike England, a country with a dole; unlike

America, which has a social safety net called welfare. Even if those who are on these programs are stigmatized, ostracized and politicized; at least they had it. Jamaica had no safety net for the poor.

THE MESSAGE

The Jamaican Reggae DJ Supercat had a hit song titled, "Cry Fi Di Youth." A song in which he chanted rhythmically, poetically, and melodically, "I will not cry for a dignitary or a big supe—I will not cry for a man in a three piece suit, nor one in a crisp pair of Clarkes boot; but I will cry, I will cry for the youth." He cried for them because many of them were born and lived in a garrison community ruled by a Don. Many had promise but lacked opportunity. Promise without opportunity can breed frustration and many of the youths in the garrison turned to the gun as a way out. International reggae singer Half Pint said, "cost of living getting higher, more sellers than buyers. Momma cry, papa cry, children cry—even the young suckling on the breast—leaving people out there so depressed."

Americans are better off economically than most of the other peoples of the world but there are also pockets of poverty here. The classic song, "The Message," by Grandmaster Flash and the Furious Five is awesome in its ability to capture what life was like for the poorest of the poor in America. As you can tell I love to take quotes from songs, so let's go to some of the poignant descriptive lyrics from, "The Message." The hook to the song is:

"Don't push me 'cause I'm close to the edge
I'm trying not to lose my head
It's like a jungle sometimes
It makes me wonder how I keep from goin' under

Broken glass everywhere
People pissin' on the stairs, you know they just don't care
I can't take the smell, can't take the noise
Got no money to move out, I guess I got no choice
Rats in the front room, roaches in the back
Junkies in the alley with a baseball bat
I tried to get away, but I couldn't get far
'Cause a man with a tow truck repossessed my car

Don't push me 'cause I'm close to the edge
I'm trying not to lose my head
It's like a jungle sometimes
It makes me wonder how I keep from goin' under"

Those lyrics are timeless; if you've ever lived in low-income projects or any low-income community you can identify with those lyrics. Greatness has to be a state of mind before it can be a state of being. I once heard Rev. Andre Cook say, "if it's not on your mind, it's not in your future." Jesus once said, "the poor you will always have with you." If greatness is a state of mind, then poverty can also be a state of mind. Don't get me wrong, there are forces and systems in this world which help to keep certain people and nations in abject poverty. India has its caste system. America has institutional racism. Many African countries are plagued by systemic corruption because of men who crown themselves presidents for life, plundering the economy through graft and greed so they and their cronies can live lavishly while their populace is underpaid and malnourished. In spite of all that, there are people who have the privilege of living in prosperous countries like America where they can apply for economic assistance, subsidized housing, and have access to a free education, but choose not to use those resources as a stepping stone to success through disciplined hard work. There are people who just want to game a system, they would rather receive a check than to work for it. They are not all relegated to one ethnic group despite what the media portrays; they come in all hues, all colors.

My mom once told me she never saw a child who cried as long and as hard as I did. But the day she was leaving, I saw one. It was my little sister who is two years younger than me. It was like a competition between us to see who could cry the loudest and the longest. I may have held the crybaby title as far as my mom was concerned, but my sister took it from me that day. It was many years ago but the shrieking sound of her ear-piercing cry for our mom is vivid to me even today. As expected, she was inconsolable. At the tender age of three, how could she understand the complexity of the situation? The economic climate in Jamaica compelled many individuals to leave the island in search of greener pastures. In many of these families, surrogates such as grandparents, aunts, uncles, older siblings, and other family members had to become the primary caretakers of the children who were left behind.

In the case of grandparents, they had to become parents all over again at a time when they should have been enjoying their empty nest. It was not uncommon for a struggling family to give one of their children to another family member. My mother had a sister who lived in the parish of St. Elizabeth; my sister Nena was sent to live with her and her husband. One of my uncles on my dad's side was given to my grandmother's cousin and her husband when he was a child. He resented the fact that he was sent to live with other family members while his eight other siblings were living at home with their parents. When he grew up, he emigrated to Canada and was estranged from his birth parents. Many years later one of his brothers, Winston, nicknamed Jill, went to live in Canada and a friend kept telling him she knew someone who looked like him. Uncle Jill worked in a hospital, but he was also a singer who performed in many reggae shows. On one occasion, he was being introduced at a show when the brother he had not seen or spoken to in years was in the audience. When he heard them introduce Winston 'Jill' Donaldson, he said, "That's my brother." Although he resented the fact he was given away, he was elated to find his brother who eventually introduced him to the rest of his siblings. My grandparents thought they were doing what was best for him and the couple, who had no children of their own. It could not have been an easy decision for my grandparents, especially my grandmother.

For my mother and countless other mothers, living in poverty was like being caught between a rock and a hard place. You can stay at home and deal with not being able to provide for your family in the manner you feel you should or split up the family by emigrating in search of a better opportunity. Someone once said, "when opportunity knocks, open the door." There are times when the door of opportunity requires great sacrifice to get to it and get through it. Leaving her children, albeit temporarily, has to be one of the most difficult decisions a mother can make. The natural instinct of a mother is to protect and care for her child. This can often mean making tough decisions which may be extremely trying in the short term but lead to long term benefits for the family.

The kids and adults in some of these families don't understand the difficulties endured by the person who emigrates. In some families, the separation causes irreparable harm; the child grows up harboring resentment towards the parent who left them in the care of other family members. Some use what they feel was abandonment as a tool for emotional blackmail and manipulation, holding it over the parent for years. Not only do they harbor resentment, but a sense of entitlement as if the parent who left them owes them for life. I've heard some who I consider to be ingrates, tell their parent they never did anything for them. I can't even imagine how that parent feels, when they gave up so much, put up with so much to help their family, only to be accused of abandoning them, and doing nothing to help them. I was not the most unselfish child growing up, but I always had some sense of the struggles my mom endured in order to help us. I didn't fully understand, but I was not oblivious to it. The fact that a person feels abandoned does not mean they were abandoned. Mitigating factors must be taken into consideration. Economics and the pursuit of a better life is a key factor for the parent who has to leave their child in order to help him. A scene from a show I watched as a child called "The Little Rascals," is an example: Spanky was about to get a spanking and his father or mother told him, "This is going to hurt me more than it hurts you." That sounds ridiculous to the child being spanked but to the parent, it is better for the child in the long run.

One of my great regrets in life, something which has always haunted me is not showing how much I appreciated the sacrifices my mom made for me. Keeping out of trouble and applying myself in school to become as successful as I could would have been a great way to do that. I had many obstacles in my way and unfortunately, I tripped over many of them which caused me to stumble and fall. As they say, hindsight is 20/20; I believe most of us, if given the chance to go back, would make better decisions in our lives. One of the many things my dad told me when I was younger has proven itself to be true. He told me what he learned from his dad, "You can't take back a spoken word or a spent coin."

TEN JOBS MON

Some people who have not had the opportunity to live in a prosperous country think the streets in America and other countries are paved with gold; they think the person who arrives in one of these countries will have instant success. They don't know the guilt and anguish felt by a loving mother who has to hear the sound of a baby daughter crying as if it is a matter of life and death. They don't understand the obstacles which must be overcome, the sacrifice of multiple menial jobs their family member has to take to pay their bills and send assistance home to their dependents. Back in the day there was a show called *In Living Color*, it had a sketch which satirized the hard-working Jamaican. The segment was called, "Hey Mon." The hard-working Jamaican was described as having ten jobs. This is a well-known caricature; while it is an exaggeration, there is some truth to it.

Many Jamaican immigrants had to work two or three jobs to help themselves and their family members back home. Some had to rent a room in someone else's house because they could not afford a place of their own. I remember a time when one of my family members sent his cousin in Jamaica some clothes, including a pair of new sneakers. When he handed him the sneakers, the cousin scoffed and chided him for giving him a pair of sneakers that were not a name brand. It was at a time when Air Jordans were at the height of popularity and very expensive. He thought anything less than Jordans was beneath him. This mindset was pervasive among many people who felt a sense of entitlement when they had a family member abroad who did their best to help feed and clothe them. You would have to walk in someone else's shoes to truly under-stand the difficulty of their journey. Not everyone is able to journey through life in an expensive pair of Jordans.

I have heard horror stories of Jamaicans who worked hard at multiple jobs in their host countries for years in order to send money home to a loved one to have a retirement home built. A comfortable place which would reflect the fruit of their labor. Some of them could not visit their home country because they overstayed the time allot-ted on their visas, or they entered the country illegally. They sent thousands of dollars to a family member or friend they considered trustworthy. Eventually when they were able to return home, they realized they had been scammed and there was no home for their retirement. Can you imagine working two, sometimes three jobs, denying yourself certain comforts and amenities in order to save for your retirement, only to find out you have been ripped off?

Some men who emigrated received a visa to do farm work. Many worked countless hours in the sun cutting sugar cane or harvesting some other crops. Many of the women had jobs commonly referred to as "live-in;" the worker lives in the home of a family during the week, taking care of children or an elderly person, and goes home on weekends. This type of care includes washing, cooking, cleaning, grocery shopping, play dates for young children, and so much more. Some women work long hours on multiple jobs and endure abuse because their employer knows they are in the country illegally. I've been watching a series on Hulu titled *Little Fires Everywhere*. The series is based on Celeste Ng's 2017 best-selling book. The main characters are Elena Richardson, played by Reese Witherspoon, and Mia Warren who is played by Kerry Washington. Both characters portray mothers from different socio-economic backgrounds. There is a scene where Elena asks Mia to work in her home. Mia uses the word "maid," while Elena describes the position as "house manager." When there is a falling out between both women, Elena says to Mia, "I thought we were friends," to which Mia responds, "White women always want to be friends with their maids." The majority of Jamaicans I know who have done home health aide or "live-in" work, including people in my own family, have done it in the homes of upper middle class or wealthy whites.

Some of these immigrants depend on their employers to file a petition for them which would allow them to have permanent resident status. With that status they could apply for the coveted American Citizenship. When the economy in the country where they live and work has a downturn, immigrants are the scapegoats. They are accused of taking jobs which belong to citizens, getting access to social and medical services they don't deserve, even blamed for the crime rate in some cities. During an election season it is not unusual to hear politicians use racist and xenophobic rhetoric to point the finger at immigrants, accusing them of being criminals. The ultimate irony is—other than Native Americans, all other groups are in America because their family members came from some other lands as immigrants. Some used a legal process, some just showed up on a ship called the Mayflower and eventually took control of the native peoples' lands.

Not all stories of immigrants doing home health aide and home attendant work are horror stories. I've heard of cases where the employer has been very loving and kind to their attendant, some have even left large sums of money to their caretaker. I have a family member who was a trusted caretaker to an elderly lady for years. She ran the lady's household affairs which included managing her accounts. The lady planned to leave her a substantial amount of money, but the lady's lawyer informed my family member that the lady's family would contest it. She ultimately received a quarter of a million dollars when the lady died.

Many other mothers and fathers in Jamaica and other islands and countries had to make a sacrificial move to help their families. Some of the countries people emigrate from are so poor, family members would practically starve to death if not for the help they receive from abroad. Children would not be able to attend school without the assistance they receive from their parent or caretaker; assistance which pays their school fees, pays for their uniforms, and allows them to eat lunch. Families would be evicted, unable to pay their rent without money being sent from abroad. I watched an interview on YouTube on a program called "Teach Dem," with Little Lenny, a well-known Jamaican dancehall DJ from the 90s. His mother had seven children, and the family lived in poverty in Kingston. One Christmas, his mother decided she was going to get all of her children some nice clothes for Christmas. The only problem was, the only money she had was the rent money. She bought Little Lenny and his siblings new clothes and shoes, and had to hide from her irate landlord.

GUN IN A BAGGY

Lenny was a very bright child who missed school on Fridays because he had to help his mother with her business selling brassieres, slips, and other commodities. Lenny was also a gifted DJ at a young age. He earned money by selling bottles he collected in the dancehalls and later, by applying his musical talents in those same dancehalls. When he gained entrance to the prestigious Kingston College high school by passing an exam called "Common Entrance," it was a time of celebration for his family. That celebration was cut short when the principal read an article in a local paper called, "The Jamaica Gleaner," that said Little Lenny was the DJ who recorded the explicit, raunchy hit song "Gun in a Baggy," and kicked Lenny out of the school. The principal accused him of dishonoring Kingston College by recording a song that disrespected women. "Gun in a baggy" means a girl has a sexually transmitted disease which is like a gun in her underwear that shoots the man who has sex with her.

Little Lenny's narrative along with others from similar backgrounds were common to many families who were split apart when one or both parents had to emigrate to America, England, or Canada in search of what is commonly referred to in America as the American Dream. Some gained entry to these wealthy countries legally through visas or by obtaining permanent residence, through a green card process. Many applied for citizenship through a naturalization process, while others stayed when their visas were up. Some decided to enter illegally, which earned them the title of illegal aliens.

America is not perfect, but one of its greatest attributes is its willingness to allow people from every nation to come here and have access to opportunities which are not available in their native lands. Yes, there are obstacles for some which are based on the color of their skin, but those obstacles notwithstanding, America still is the place which gives an individual his or her best chance to succeed. This is truly a great nation, with all its shortcomings. If asked what makes America great, some would say the economy, some would say its military, some would say its form of government. I agree with all of the above, but one of the first things I would say is: America is great because it is the land of opportunity. A great economy, great freedoms that a democratic government offers citizens and non-citizens, or great military protection is meaningless to a person who does not have access to opportunity.

America is great because it gives people of all nations access to greatness. The playing field is not always level but with creativity and ingenuity you can overcome the hurdles on the field. Slavery and the Jim Crow era were brutal times in American history, one of the effects of segregation is that it denied that access to its citizens of African descent, whether born or naturalized. I had a love-hate relationship with America when I was younger because of the way I was treated, despite what Thomas Jefferson wrote about "all men being created equal." Growing up I was taught, "never bite the hand that feeds you," so I guess I've always loved America for "feeding" me opportunity. The older I get, the more I love her. I guess she is like a vintage wine, the older she gets, the more value she has.

MOTHERS—THE CROWN JEWEL OF CREATION

My mom made a great sacrifice and did a noble thing, but a child does not understand why a parent is there one moment and gone the next. The child cries because he or she does not want to be left behind. I was no different. My grandparents were loving and kind, I had other siblings, but Mommy was gone, and I could not understand why. At some point my crying stopped and I settled down to life as it was, but the seed of abandonment was planted, and it would produce some terrible fruit in the years to come. One such bad fruit was bedwetting, long past the time it should have ceased. There was also the fruit of an inferiority complex from being ridiculed because I spoke, dressed and looked different. When I grew older, I always made sure I was impeccably dressed and spoke properly when I went out in public.

My mom was the quintessential hard-working American immigrant. She worked the three-to-eleven shift at Memorial Sloan Kettering Hospital in Manhattan. I remember the night she came home and told us the great Bob Marley was in the hospital and he had cancer. She also sewed in the mornings and on weekends. She was able to save enough money to purchase a two-family home with a basement. Twice a year she sent a barrel to Jamaica, full of clothes and toys for us. New clothes and toys from "foreign," the name that is used to refer to America and other prosperous countries outside of Jamaica. The gifts gave me a burst of joy and euphoria, but it was short-lived because they could not replace my mother. My book *Great Women* is a tribute to women in general but more specifically to the two women who have had the greatest impact on my life. Monica Maxwell, the woman who birthed me and sacrificed to give me a better life, and Paulette Donaldson, the wife who endured the hardships of my metamorphosis and never ceased to be the "Good Thing," the "Help Meet," that her Creator created her to be.

I heard a parable of a piglet asking his mother why her nose was so long. The mother told him, "Son, keep growing and one day you will understand." When we left the lights on or threw away food that should have been eaten, my mom told us, "Just wait, one day you will have kids." We knew about kids in other countries who were starving. We saw the pictures on TV of kids in Africa who were skinny from malnutrition, with flies all around them. I always wondered why Africa needed aid when it is the continent with the most natural resources. Mom explained, there were some things we would understand only through experience. Years later I found myself scolding my own children for leaving the lights on or wasting food. When I did, I could hear the words of my mother and I understood firsthand what she tried to teach us. We have a saying in Jamaica, "he who feels it, knows it."

Sad to say I did not have the same track record of sacrifice that my mother does. My wife is more qualified to tell that story than I am. She had to leave two young children in Jamaica to seek a better life in America. I had choices they did not have. I could have chosen to get my education before starting to father children so I could better provide for them, but I chose not to. Actions cause reactions and choices have consequences. There are actions I took, choices I made that had repercussions that I have to deal with to this day. I am both thankful and grateful that I am wiser and more disciplined now. The older I get, the more appreciative I am of the greatness that is in my mom. She could have settled for the environment she was born into, but she made a choice to be better, for herself and for her family. She had a desire to achieve and succeed and was willing to take action to make her dream a reality. For that I love her, and I am eternally grateful and indebted to her.

CHAPTER 3

Bullied on Sight

IN 1776, AT THE START of the American Revolution, Thomas Jefferson wrote some words in the U.S. Declaration of Independence that I consider to be some of the greatest words ever written:

"We hold these truths to be self-evident, that all men are created equal, that they are endowed by their creator with certain unalienable rights, that among these are life, liberty and the pursuit of happiness. That to secure these rights, Governments are instituted among men, deriving their just powers from the consent of the governed. That whenever any form of government becomes destructive of these ends, it is the right of the people to alter or to abolish it, and to institute new Government, laying its foundation on such principles and organizing its powers in such form, as to them shall seem most likely to effect their safety and happiness."

The first time I read those words, I knew they were special. But it didn't take long for me to find out that words on paper can be lofty and idealistic, but they do not always translate to reality for everyone. The justification for the thirteen American colonies' rebellion against the control of the monarchy in Great Britain was succinctly laid out in the Declaration of Independence. While the colonies were ready and willing to go to war for freedom, wealthy intellectuals—leaders of the revolution including Jefferson, had men, women, and children enslaved because of the color of their skin. How do you stand behind the words declaring all men equal, with an unalienable right to life and liberty while keeping people in bondage? You do it by declaring that a black man was only three-fifths of a man.

Thomas Jefferson, the third president of the United States, owned more than 600 African American slaves throughout his adult life and freed only two while he was alive, with another seven freed after his death. Jefferson consistently spoke out against the international slave trade, which was outlawed while he was President, while he advocated gradual emancipation and colonization of domestic slaves. Common for his times, Jefferson believed blacks were inherently inferior to whites and thought it was best the two races remained segregated. It is obvious to me that Jefferson was referring to all *white* men being created equal and endowed by their creator with certain inalienable rights. This is evidenced by the fact that blacks did not receive equal treatment. A bloody civil war would have to be fought to liberate them from slavery. At this very moment there is an attempt to roll back some of the freedoms gained through the Emancipation Proclamation and the period of Reconstruction; one of the most fundamental of these freedoms is the right to vote. "Slavery is not abolished until the black man has the ballot," Frederick Douglass famously said.[2]

My mom had seven children; four girls and three boys. My oldest brother was shot to death in Jamaica in 2007. When my brother-in-law Ian called me and gave me the news, I was in shock. One week later, my wife received news that her brother had died suddenly in a hotel in Jamaica while on vacation. It was a surreal experience, a nightmare I thought we would simply awaken from, but it was a reality that we had to deal with.

TROUBLE DON'T LAST ALWAYS

For inspiration and strength, I draw on the wise sayings I was taught growing up, sayings like, "don't air your dirty laundry in public." So, there is some reticence on my part in sharing certain things. But, for the sake of transparency in telling my story I feel compelled to tell it all; the good, the bad, and the ugly. Transparency in telling and writing can be cathartic. It challenges you to come to terms with your feelings and deal with issues that have laid dormant for years. Some family secrets have to be revealed, in the hope that revelation will help others who have been bound, trapped in a prison of toxic secrecy. There is a Greek translation of the word revelation, it is "apokalupsis," which comes from the root words "apo" and "kalýptein" meaning to uncover or reveal. Taking the cover off some things that have been hidden or swept under the rug is extremely difficult, but necessity dictates they be discussed.

Carol Anthony Wallace was his name, though he preferred "Carl" for obvious reasons; may his soul have eternal rest. This is my wish and prayer, because his soul did not have much rest when he was alive. He was a troubled soul from the time we lived in Jamaica. "Man that is born of a woman is of few days, and full of trouble" (JOB 14:1 KJV).

Bipolar disorder was not diagnosed back then, but in retrospect I would say that is what he suffered from. He became a Rastafarian and was radical, militant, and prone to violence at a moment's notice. He told me the slaves that were brought to Jamaica and other parts of the Caribbean were the ones who could not be broken because they were from the militant tribes in Africa. I didn't know if that was historically correct, but it sounded good to me because my eldest brother said it, and because I was starved for news about blacks who were willing to fight against racism and oppression. He would definitely be what you would call a conspiracy theorist today. He always spoke about a Maccabee Bible being the true Bible and instead of Jesus he praised King Selassie.

I learned later through my own studies that the Maccabees were a Jewish sect—a group of Jewish rebel warriors who took control of Judea, which at the time was part of the Seleucid Empire. They reasserted the Jewish religion, partly by forced conversion, and expanded the boundaries of Judea by conquest. Carol was unwavering in his belief that the King James Version of the Bible was not the real version.

If you had a disagreement with Carol, he would pull a knife or a gun on you in a minute. He was prone to erupt violently at the slightest perceived disrespect. The memory has not faded with the passing of time due to the traumatic nature of the event. It was night and Carol was in the house obviously under the influence of alcohol and agitated. I was not one to hold my tongue, at times to my own detriment. In a burst of emotional frustration, I said something to him and before I knew it, he pushed me down, grabbed a pair of scissors and raised his hands over me. I grabbed his hand, stricken by fear and terror. A couple of my other siblings were able to pull him off me. If not for their intervention, I have no doubt he would have plunged the scissors into me.

PAIN LAND

We were born and lived in a tumultuous and violent area of Kingston, more specifically Thirteen Spanish Town Road, Waltham Park Road commonly referred to as The Waltham. My brother ran with some guys from Pain Avenue, also known as Pain Land. A fitting name for the suffering many of the residents had to endure. I've heard of lucky seven, but fate would have it that I would be born in thirteen, not a number that is associated with good things. I'm not superstitious, but I guess there is a reason why many buildings don't have a thirteenth floor.

On the eve of getting his opportunity to fly to America, my brother was arrested for trying to pick someone's pocket. He was locked up at Central Police Station. My dad knew a good attorney named Richard Small whose father was a high court judge. Attorney Small attended many of the socialist lectures attended by my dad and they became good friends. My Dad and my grandmother Edith went to court and Attorney Small represented my brother and explained to the judge that he had received his papers to join his mother in America. Justice is supposed to be blind, but being connected to a good lawyer whose father is a high court judge does not hurt. My grandmother asked my dad how he was going to pay the lawyer and he told her attorney Small was his friend, so he was not charged. Still, my grandmother gave my dad one hundred American dollars to give him—a decent amount of money at the time.

TRAUMA FROM THE DRAMA

When my brother came to America his troubles were magnified; he had access to guns and alcohol, a lethal combination for him. When he was sober, he was one of the nicest people you could meet, he would give you the shirt off his back. But when he was intoxicated, it was a Jekyll and Hyde business. He was feared in Corona where we lived. I never shared with him the trouble I had because I knew if I did, he would respond by shooting. Quite honestly some Jamaicans are enamored with guns. There was a Jamaican man who rented the upstairs apartment from my mom. He had some beef with some people in the neighborhood and they made the mistake of coming to the house to call him out—when he came out, he came out shooting. My brother was no different, he hid his gun in the basement; whenever he ran down there in a moment of anger, I knew it was on and popping. One night I was standing in the front of the house and I could hear shouting. When I looked up there were a couple of guys running down our street and behind them was my brother on a bicycle shooting at them. It was crazy. It is only by the grace of God that people didn't attack our house because of all the shenanigans he got into in the neighborhood. My mom and grandmother loved him though, and did everything they could to help him.

Most families have at least one member who keeps Mom up late at night. God help the mother who has two or more children like that. In Jamaica we use the term, "a pickney wey mek ar ban ar belly," a child who keeps her stomach tied, who keeps her on her knees. I know what my brother put my mother through. She put up her house to bail him out when he got arrested. He would go in her bag and take her car keys and drive her car without her permission. Most of the time he was driving under the influence of alcohol. I remember one night he brought back the station wagon, it was smashed from some accident he had. The lengths a mother will go to in order to help a wayward child are unfathomable. In my opinion, a woman is God's greatest creation because of her ability to conceive, carry, and birth—her ability to risk life and limb in order to nurture her offspring. When others have written her beloved child off, she continues to stand by them. God's love for His children is incomparable, but if I was to compare it to anything, I would compare it to the love of a mother for a child. A mother's love is the closest we can get as fallible beings to unconditional love. There are people who are estranged from their mother, but even if a mother never did anything else for her child, she conceived, endured the physical and emotional changes of her trimesters, and endured the labor pains to give birth. She is a life-giver and for that act alone she should be celebrated.

MOMMA'S BABY, POPPA'S MAYBE

I loved my brother, but he was a terror to live with. As I reflect on those times, it is a wonder I made it out alive and in my right mind. He contributed heavily to a toxic home atmosphere and there was no place of solace for me. Trouble in the house, trouble around my neighborhood, and trouble when I left the neighborhood to go to school. I cried when I heard Carol was going to be deported back to Jamaica. It was at a time when people were not deported as quickly as they are today. You had to be a serious recidivist for them to deport you and he was. He was going right back to Galloway Road off The Waltham and that was not good. He was gone from that area for many years but not much changed in terms of economic opportunity. It was still a dangerous area to live.

Although I cried, a part of me was relieved because living with him was like being on the roller coaster at Coney Island. He worked at a fast food joint back in the day and some nights when he came home from work, he would bring me food, sit on the bed and talk to me. It was cool having an older brother to speak to, but the next day he could morph into a different creature. He was not on any mind or mood-altering medication but in retrospect he should have been. Anyone who is dealing with or has dealt with a family member who suffers from bipolar disorder or paranoid schizophrenia will tell you about the stress level, the tears they cry, the difficult decisions they have to make as they watch their loved one completely deteriorate right before their eyes.

Certain individuals are genetically predisposed to mental illness in the same manner some are predisposed to heart disease, cancer, etc. My Grand Aunt Teacher Barnes, sister to my Grandmother Edith, had a son named Koufa who had a brilliant mind; I didn't know it at the time, but he suffered from paranoid schizophrenia. My dad told me Teacher Barnes once asked him to take Koufa to one of the lectures he attended at UWI. He said on one occasion after a lecture when they were walking to get a cab home, Koufa's behavior became erratic and he had a difficult time getting him to his house. He lived at home with Teacher Barnes and attended Calabar High School when he was able to function mentally. She owned a beautiful home on Oakland Road with a prep school on the property. I remember when I had to take his lunch to him during the lunch hour when I was at her prep school. As I went up the stairs and approached the door, I was shaking. I was a child, but I knew there was something strange about him. Whenever he opened the door, he had a strange look on his face. He never spoke too much to me, just took the lunch from me, said thank you, and closed the door.

One day I was sitting in the classroom looking out the window and there he was in the yard, dressed in his customary khaki suit like a schoolboy. But there was no book in his hand, no pen, nor paper. There was a pot on top of a makeshift stove cooking. I stared at him and at the fire. I'd seen wood and coal fires being used for cooking on many occasions. After all, my beloved grandmother Edith Maxwell utilized those means for cooking her food. But there was something Promethean about him and the fire he stoked. Not long after, he burned his mom's beautiful home and her school to the ground. He was my mother's first cousin, making him my brother Carol's second cousin. Did they inherit a certain gene for mental illness, a certain fascination for burning things? I'm not a scientist, so I don't know. In one of his many violent outbursts, Carol grabbed some paint thinner, threw it on the floor and tried to burn our house down. For years I could see the orange flames emanating from the floor as my mom and my older siblings scrambled to put the fire out. Someone once said, "the more things change, the more they stay the same." My youngest son battles with schizophrenia, so I know these things are generational and not merely coincidental.

It's hard to imagine what it must be like to be deported to an impoverished community after living in America for years. Some people in the community look upon the deportee with disgust and disdain because they feel they would have better utilized the opportunity. I supported Carol as best I could by sending him money. I tried to convince him to stop drinking when I visited but living in a war zone made it tough for him. His friend had a bar on Berwick which he frequented. One day some gunmen entered the bar and killed his friend and two women. I heard that my brother was coming home from work and was shot to death because he was friends with the bar owner. The memory and the effects of trauma do not go away as soon as the drama, the incident which causes the trauma, is taken away; hence the term, Post Traumatic Stress Disorder. This condition is mostly associated with individuals who have been in a war, but it is not exclusive to them. When you are exposed to certain traumatic things as a child, the memories and their effects can last for years, and sometimes for the duration of the individual's life if there is no help. A rape may last for minutes but the trust issues the victim has to deal with can last for many years. It can affect their relationships with other people. There is a frigidity, an inability to have intimacy because the memory of the trauma is always there. If you've grown up around violence from childhood, it has an impact on your outlook on life, the decisions you make. Children learn by imitating the speech and actions of the people they are around. If their early childhood environment is full of violence, the likelihood of them becoming violent increases. We are all products of our environment. I came home from incarceration with a strong mind, but to this day I don't like to hear a door slammed because it reminds me of the times when my iron cell door was shut.

The longest verse in The Message By Grand Master Flash sums it up best:

"A child is born with no state of mind
Blind to the ways of mankind
God is smilin' on you but he's frownin' too
Because only God knows what you'll go through
You'll grow in the ghetto livin' second-rate
And your eyes will sing a song called deep hate
The places you play and where you stay
Looks like one great big alleyway
You'll admire all the number-book takers
Thugs, pimps and pushers and the big money-makers
Drivin' big cars, spendin' twenties and tens
And you'll wanna grow up to be just like them, huh
Smugglers, scramblers, burglars, gamblers
Pickpocket peddlers, even panhandlers
You say I'm cool, huh, I'm no fool
But then you wind up droppin' outta high school
Now you're unemployed, all non-void
Walkin' round like you're Pretty Boy Floyd
Turned stick-up kid, but look what you done did
Got sent up for a eight-year bid
Now your manhood is took and you're a Maytag
Spend the next two years as a undercover fag
Bein' used and abused to serve like hell
'Til one day, you was found hung dead in the cell
It was plain to see that your life was lost
You was cold and your body swung back and forth
But now your eyes sing the sad, sad song
Of how you lived so fast and died so young."

I am number five, the youngest of the three sons with two sisters who are younger. My mother was able to send for all of her children to live with her in America but not all at the same time. The older siblings came first, then the younger. When it was my time to travel, my father took me and my brother to King Street and blessed us with two tailor-made suits for our trip. It was always a big deal for family and friends when someone in their midst was leaving to live in America. It represented a chance, an opportunity for better and greater. The Jamaican mindset and I am sure the mindset of other ethnic groups is, all we need is a chance for a better life. The opportunity to work and send my children to school. We don't need handouts, welfare, we only need a chance, an opportunity. Thanks to my mom and her aunt who helped her get her chance and opportunity; me and my siblings were getting ours. The younger among us did not fully comprehend what it meant for us to go to America. We were caught up in the excitement, the euphoria of our elders.

My trip to live abroad would represent many firsts for me. My first time on a plane, my first time leaving Jamaica, my first winter, and some other firsts that would set me on a course of self-destructive behavior and decision-making. I was excited about being reunited with my mother, but ill-prepared for some of the things I would face in America: the land of the free and the home of the brave.

I'M A LEGAL ALIEN

Leaving a city like Kingston and moving to New York City was a culture shock. Corona is the name of the area where my mother lived. It was a low-income neighborhood in Queens, New York where black Americans, West Indians, and Hispanic people lived. I found out early on that being black in a neighborhood where other black people lived didn't mean you would be accepted because of your shared skin color. I was made acutely aware that I was different and would not be accepted because I spoke with a deep West Indian accent and did not dress like the cool kids. They were the fly guys and girls, they wore Pro Keds and Converse, but I was mocked mercilessly for wearing sneakers they called "skips." They wore gabardine from Delancey Street while I had to settle for polyester from Goodwill. Some of them achieved their stylish attire by stealing and robbing people. Like any other child, I wanted to fit in and be accepted. If there is something about a child which causes them stand out, they want to be celebrated not hated. The very name "alien," which was used to describe immigrants, encapsulates how they are viewed by the indigenous people—something that is strange. People are intrigued but not necessarily enamored by aliens. The difference in one person can cause another to feel threatened. When people are threatened, they go to great lengths to protect themselves from the perceived threat, whether or not the threat is credible. People in power who want to enforce a divide-and-conquer paradigm to maintain control will often use mass media to spread rumors about a particular group to foster animosity.

Growing up in New York meant I would find out what the multi-talented and versatile singer and DJ Shine meant when he sang the hook to his song,

> *"I'm an alien, I'm a legal alien*
> *I'm a Jamaican in New York"*

I had to deal with bullying in school and in my neighborhood. I was picked on and teased mercilessly by other kids and wondered why I had to leave Jamaica. At the outset, the American dream was looking like a nightmare. Where were the streets paved with gold? Instead of gold I saw empty bottles of Wild Irish Rose, Boone's Farm, and Mad Dog 2020; cheap wines drunk by the winos who hung out on corners.

I had another problem I had to deal with. My father was not in the home, he could not leave Jamaica with my mom because the permanent resident status she received did not include her husband. My mom filed for him and he arrived in 1976, four years later. His arrival should have been a joyous occasion, but that was not the case. My mother had a great deal of anger and resentment in her heart because of the things she suffered. I remember how short-lived the joy of finally having my father in our home was. The first night he came, there was an argument, and my mother asked him to leave. I was fourteen and it was another moment in a series of devastating things I experienced. My father was taken in by my uncle and his girlfriend. He eventually remarried a very nice lady who had children.

With no adult male role model in the home, my older brother battled mental and emotional issues which caused him to drink, and when he was drunk he was a violent individual. When we came home from school, Mommy was not home because of her shift at the hospital. The atmosphere in our house was very tough at times, but the atmosphere outside was tougher. I was catching hell from the bullies in the neighborhood which built up hatred, anger, and resentment in my heart. Bullying has been in the news because some kids commit suicide as a result of being bullied. The anger deepened in my heart when it was time to go to school, in a predominantly white neighborhood where I soon learned it didn't matter to many of the white kids who was an American black, a West Indian black, or other. In their eyes we were all niggers who needed to go back to Africa or wherever we came from.

The blacks in the neighborhood used to say, "go back on your banana boat," and the whites used to just say, "go back." There didn't seem to be any place for me to fit in. When I watched TV, I saw a man called Tarzan swinging through the jungle and beating up a bunch wild-looking Africans. On the news, I heard about a country called South Africa where blacks lived like indentured servants. I heard about a freedom fighter named Nelson Mandela who was in prison because he was an advocate for social justice in the land of his forefathers. I couldn't believe it. I was catching hell in America, and the black man was catching hell in Africa, the land of his ancestors. I felt completely alone.

No single group has a monopoly on bigotry and hatred. Years ago, I came to understand what is commonly referred to as the "crab in the barrel" mentality. One crab in a barrel will attempt to climb on top and over another crab in a futile attempt to get out, oblivious to the fact that the crab master waits to put the crab back in the barrel, or worse, into a pot of boiling water. You would think people who face a common enemy would band together to overcome, but on the contrary many of the oppressed peoples of the world wind up oppressing each other; succumbing to the divide-and-conquer principle. As an immigrant child, I suffered at the hands of both people who looked like me and people who did not look like me. Hatred is a condition of the heart, not of a person's skin color. It is a learned behavior, perpetrated by ignorant people who want to maintain a system where others are subservient.

Some Jamaicans were not only the victims, they were the perpetrators at times. It was not uncommon for me to hear some Jamaicans use the term "Yankee," as a derogatory way of describing black Americans. They described some of them as people who were lazy, who preferred welfare instead of work. That is a mindset I never adopted, because I did not see the wisdom in fighting against each other when we had a common enemy who posed a more existential threat to us. As far as I was concerned, that was just common sense. Once I started to educate myself on African History, colonialism, the slave trade, and the Jim Crow system which was the "black-lash" to the freedom given to the slaves, I knew I had to become a voice crying in the wilderness for justice. Instead of settling for an Anglicized miseducation which glamorized European civilization while making no mention of the great contributions made by blacks in Africa and in the diaspora, I would do the research necessary to educate my mind and free my soul. I was spurred on by the slogan of The United Negro College Fund, "A mind is a terrible thing to waste."

Reading became my means of elevating my mind and escaping the sadness and despair I felt. My mom grew up in a family which stressed education, that idea was drummed into our minds at a young age. I remember the times when we wanted to go outside to play with other kids and my mom's response was go and find something to read or watch Channel Thirteen. I remember when she bought us a set of Encyclopedia Britannica. I read voraciously, understanding that an uneducated mind was a mind that could be kept in bondage. The lyrics from Bob Marley's "Redemption Song" rang in my ears,

"Emancipate yourself from mental slavery
None but our self can free our minds
Have no fear for atomic energy
'Cause none of them can stop the time
How long shall they kill our prophets
While we stand aside and look?
Some say it's just a part of it
We've got to fulfill di book"

A DREAM OR A NIGHTMARE

My choices for reading were normally books which addressed the issues I dealt with, such as bullying and racism. *World's Great Men of Color* by J.A Rogers was one of my favorites. I read Dick Gregory's book, *Nigger*, Toni Morrison's novel *Song of Solomon* and was intrigued by the character "Milkman Dead" and the gang called, "The Seven Days." The Honorable Marcus Garvey's mantra, "Africa for the Africans at home and abroad" became my battle cry. My cry got louder when someone introduced me to the writings and recorded speeches of the son of a Garvey follower by the name of Malcolm Little. The world would come to know him as Malcolm X. If allowed to fester, feelings of hatred, anger, and bitterness can cause an individual to adopt extreme positions and I was no different. Malcolm's slogan against racial and social injustice, "By any means necessary," became my other mantra. I looked at the cops who patrolled my neighborhood through the lens of hatred and disdain because they were more like occupiers than officers of the law. There were some criminals and gangsters in the neighborhood so law enforcement was necessary, but the solution would certainly not come from patrolmen who behaved more like Ku Klux Klansmen than officers of the law. King Martin had a dream because the black experience was a nightmare. I followed X because it didn't seem like Martin's dream could become a reality through non-violent means. I felt a connection to the teachings of X because of his connection to Marcus Garvey by way of his father. Once again, the revolutionary spirit in me connected with revolutionary thoughts and ideas about racism and how to combat it.

It always surprises me when someone is surprised that a black person would vehemently resist racism and police brutality by any means necessary. It was quite acceptable for the people in the Thirteen Colonies to fight the War of Independence against Britain for taxation without representation. Their rebellion and insurrection against monarchical rule are taught in schools, celebrated every Fourth of July. Would anyone be surprised by a Jewish person resisting a Nazi? Why should the idea of a black person speaking out against racial tyranny be surprising? Why aren't black and white children in America taught about Toussaint Louverture, the Haitian general who led the Haitian Revolution? We need the truth, the whole truth, and nothing but the truth, so help us God! People should know there is more to Haiti than what you hear in the media about the island being the poorest in the Western Hemisphere. Black history shouldn't be a mystery; it shouldn't be reduced to a single month on the calendar. Black history is a rich part of human history which goes far beyond slavery in America and the West Indies.

> *"A people without the knowledge of their past history, origin and culture is like a tree without Roots"*
>
> —Marcus Garvey

THE PO PO

It was a summer night in 1977. Me, my two younger sisters, and my friend Charles were walking to the store. When we reached the middle of the block, the lights went out and we found ourselves in the midst of a blackout. It was both scary and fun at the same time. Instead of turning back and heading to the house, we kept walking until we were at Northern Boulevard. Before we could turn the corner, a car pulled up and a white guy jumped out and told us not to move. Shortly thereafter he was joined by two more white guys in plain clothes. It didn't take me long to realize they were undercover cops. Why were they telling us not to move and to get up against the wall? I thought we were in a free country? All we wanted to do was go to the store and get some candy and popsicles and get home before we were robbed. People tried to rob me in broad daylight before so a blackout would be the time you would get robbed if you were caught off guard. We weren't looters or burglars, opportunists looking to steal someone else's property, we were not raised that way. But that didn't matter to those cops. We were black and there was a blackout, so we had to be up to no good. It didn't matter to them that my younger sisters were with us. They wanted to make sure we knew who was in charge, even though that was pretty evident by looking at their badges and guns.

I was fifteen at the time and had a very smart mouth. Before I could ask them, "what for," my friend asked the question and the cop's response was to punch my friend in the eye. As I stood in shock, my sisters cried out, "Leave him alone!" They jumped into the car almost as fast as they jumped out at us and drove off. It all happened so fast. My friend had his hand over his eye, and when we arrived back at the house his eye was swollen shut. We felt power-less, who should we call? The police? It wasn't the stick-up kids we should have been concerned about; it was the po po. The most dangerous criminals were the ones with a gun, a badge, and a Blue Wall of Silence to protect them. The swelling in Charles' eye even-tually went down, but my heart swelled that night with hatred for the white cops who hurt my friend with no provocation. A seed of mistrust was planted that night and it would be nourished by other encounters with the police. I had heard and read about the brutal-ity of racist cops in the south during the Jim Crow era, but I was in the north. Wasn't it the north where people fought against slavery? It didn't take me long to realize that many whites in the north were just as racist as their counterparts in the south.

YUSUF AND EMMETT – NEVER FORGET!

Yusuf Hawkins learned about racism the hard way. He was a 16 year old teenager from East New York, Brooklyn. On August 23rd, 1989, he was shot to death in a predominantly Italian-American work-ing-class neighborhood called Bensonhurst. Yusuf and three of his friends were attacked by a crowd of white youths, some of whom were wielding baseball bats. One of them, Joey Fama, pulled a gun and shot him twice in the chest. Yusuf had gone to Bensonhurst that night with his three friends to inquire about a used car that was for sale. Fama and the gang of murderous marauders were lying in wait for a black youth they believed had dated a neighborhood girl. Yusuf and his friends were oblivious to the fact they were walking into a hornet's nest of racist murderers. That was not the first time some white boys suffering from penis envy would murder a black male because of paranoia that the black man was taking his woman. Fifty years earlier on August 25th, 1955, 14-year-old Emmet Till was brutally beaten and lynched after being falsely accused of offending a white woman named Carolyn Bryant in her family's grocery store. Decades later, she admitted she had lied about her story.

The more things change, the more they stay the same. Decades after leaving New York and returning for a visit, I stopped on Northern Boulevard to greet the cousin of a childhood friend. He looked like he had fallen on hard times. I could tell that he was a crack addict, but I was not going to act like I did not know him because that is not the kind of person I am. When he called to me, I walked over and started speaking with him, and before I knew what was going on some cops jumped out of a car and told me, "Don't move." One of them frisked me and searched my pockets, and when he did not find anything he left. I was the victim of racial profiling because I stopped to greet someone I grew up with, someone I had not seen in years. This racial profiling was not the idea of some rogue cops in the police department, it was the official policy instituted by the mayor.

Hate is a very strong word, one that I don't like to use. On that night of the blackout of 1977, I felt hatred, disdain, and disgust for those cops. An unjustified assault against my friend for no reason other than the cop had a badge, a gun, and the power to do so. It is definitely wrong to judge an entire demographic of people based on the actions of a few, but I was on guard when I saw a white man in a blue police uniform. Because the experiences I had with them were life threatening, I didn't get the chance to distinguish between the good, the bad, and the ugly. I put them all in the same category: the oppressors. They took an oath to do a dangerous and legitimate job, but some of them became more crooked than the criminals they were assigned to catch.

My blood boiled when I heard about Eleanor Bumpurs and Amadou Diallo, two victims of police violence who were killed in or around their homes for simple misunderstandings. I thought, "you reap what you sow," when I heard on the news that Larry Davis had shot his way out of a police trap in the Bronx. A brother could not catch a break. Bullied and harassed in the place I called home by people who were supposed to be my peers, attacked and threatened by others when I left the neighborhood to go to school, and now the ones who took an oath to protect became the persecutors. Another event would transpire when I turned sixteen that would cement my hateful mindset. It would embed in my heart a steely determination to fight back and adopt a philosophy of death before dishonor. This philosophy would cause me to put my life on the line in many instances. I was convinced I would not live to see the age of thirty.

"Life inna de ghetto it no easy," is a common lyric you hear when you listen to reggae songs coming out of Kingston. As rough as things could be in certain parts of Kingston in terms of violence, it was no easier in America as a black man. It has caused me to adopt the concept of "living while black." For those who would say, "go back where you came from," I say there is no country I can go to that has not been damaged by the racism of colonialism. When all the riches earned from slavery in America and the West Indies are returned to the land and people it was stolen from, then you will have the right to tell us where to go. Until then, shut your mouth.

CHAPTER 4

Middleman to Darkness

AS I APPROACHED MY HIGH school years, I was in full rebellion mode. My closest friends at the time were two Americans and one Barbadian. In high school the Americans knew I was a Jamaican; although I dressed like one of the boys in the hood, my Americanized accent was tinged with a little Jamaican patois.

MAN POWER

I was able to shed my Goodwill clothes for a more socially acceptable style. Instead of the skips I was ridiculed for wearing in junior high, I now had Pumas and pleated gabardine pants with the thread stitching that ran down each side and a different color in the middle. I don't remember if I had the Cortefiel coat with the fur on the collar, but still I was starting to make a fashion statement. The money came from a summer job I was able to get at "Man Power," a building on 103rd, and from Northern Boulevard, which had a program that gave summer jobs to young people. I couldn't wait to get my working papers as a teenager so I could earn some money and go shopping on Delancey Street like the bad boys, burglars, and stick-up kids in Corona.

The Jamaicans in Flushing High School stuck together. Many of them used the term "Yankee Bwoy" and "Yankee Gal" to describe the black Americans. Once when I opened my mouth to speak patois one of the Jamaican girls laughed, she told me I "sounded funny." Leaving Jamaica at a young age and trying to fit into a culture where I was not welcomed made me eager to rediscover my Jamaican roots. The words "roots" and "culture" were key to the Jamaican mindset, yet I had forgotten my roots and practically lost my culture. I was in high school, but still trapped in a proverbial no man's land and determined to have my cultural roots restored. I had no clue where my family originated from in Africa, but Jamaican Roots and Culture was sufficient for me. This rediscovery would take place on my first trip back to Jamaica since my departure for America.

SEEK AND YOU SHALL FIND

After high school graduation, I prepared to start at Queens College, City University Of New York. I had to start in the SEEK Program. According to the Queens College website, this program is "designed to reach qualified high school graduates who might not attend college otherwise. The program starts during the summer, with intensive workshops for matriculating freshmen who did not pass portions of the CUNY Assessment Test. During their first semester, SEEK participants are organized into learning communities— groups who take at least three courses together and develop their own informal support network. Supplemental instruction covers all the first-year classes and some upper-level courses; free tutoring is available. Staff counselors help students apply for financial aid and address personal, social, and career issues."[3]

I was smart enough in high school to have gotten into Queens College without a prerequisite program like SEEK, but I didn't work hard enough on my studies. I enjoyed the SEEK program though, there were some talented lecturers, adjunct professors, and tenured professors there. The major I chose was political science, because I was considering a future in law. It was at Queens College that my mind was further enlightened, as I was introduced to works like Ernest Hemingway's *The Sun Also Rises*, Toni Morrison's *The Bluest Eye*, William Shakespeare's *Macbeth*, and many others.

It was also at Queens College in a Poli Sci 1 class that I heard the brilliant political scientist and professor emeritus Andrew Hacker say, built into the American system is a right that many white men feel they have, no matter how low they are on the socio-economic ladder. They feel justified in calling a black man a boy, even if that black man has earned a PhD. When I heard this, I was about eighteen or nineteen. I said, "WOW, a white man willing to tell it like it I-S is." I didn't have to have a PhD to know he was telling the truth. There were several Jewish students in the class and a few blacks. Both the issues of apartheid and Israeli/Palestinian relations were heatedly discussed. I did more listening than speaking because my Jamaican blood boiled at the mere mention of a racist ideology like apartheid. I had heard about being a red-blooded American, but I was a hot-blooded Jamaican.

MS. LIBERTY

Learning about apartheid and the practice of racist whites forcing black South Africans to live in Bantustans in their own country was insane to me. I was pro-Malcolm and not into Martin at the time. It was bad enough to be black and catch hell in America and Europe, but also in Africa where the Black man came from? I knew of no European city where black people were in charge and whites were relegated to living in squalor in ghettos. A black person could barely get elected to any major office in America—the land of the free, home of the brave. You would think after hundreds of years of free slave labor from blacks, they would have more of a say in what happens economically and politically in America. People of other nations were able to arrive here, assimilate, and excel, but hurdles were placed in front of black people to make it difficult. Black people built this country on their backs and were here years before immigrants from other European countries, yet they were victimized by the divide-and-conquer strategy. Every other immigrant group could come and hate on black people.

The statue of the woman with the torch at Ellis Island may be named Liberty, but her message came with an asterisk as far as I was concerned. "Give me your tired, your poor, your huddled masses yearning to breathe free, the wretched refuse of your teeming shore. Send these, the homeless, tempest-tost to me, I lift my lamp beside the golden door!" These are lofty words indeed, as long as they apply to all people irrespective of the color of their skin. Once I was speaking to one of my cousins who grew up in England about some of the injustices in the world and he said, "At least we have the queen," to which I responded, "You can keep her." No disrespect to Queen E, she seems to be a nice old lady, I just need to know if the diamonds in her tiara were stolen from Africa during colonial times.

With everything I had seen and learned, my thinking was that Africa had to be liberated by any means necessary. My Pan-Africanist leanings didn't start when I came to America; it was in my DNA from the time my grandmother Edith Maxwell attended the UNIA meetings and my grandfather taught my father history. I remembered reading about Jomo Kenyatta and the Mau Mau Rebellion against colonial rule in Kenya and thinking, we need more freedom fighters like him. My problem with many of the African leaders is this: like Fidel Castro, they start out fighting for a noble cause but once they seize power, it intoxicates them, and they repress the people to stay in power. Another saying I heard at Queens College was, "power corrupts, and absolute power corrupts absolutely." At the time, I was still heated from watching Alex Haley's television miniseries *Roots*. When professor Hacker made that statement about the American system, it put a lot of things in perspective for me and I never forgot it.

I believe it was my freshman year of college when I took my first trip back to Jamaica. The eighties had begun and sound systems like Killamanjaro, Youthman Promotion, and King Jammy were cranked up in the dance halls; DJs chanting, singers singing to the rhythm. Men and women of all ages wined slowly and rhythmically to the bassline as Red Stripe, Heineken, and Dragon Stout flowed. I heard Michael Palmer sing, "no more lean boot me dun wid it, no more board house no pit toilet." His good friend Half Pint said, "Ease up missa landlord me caan tek de pressure inna yu yaad. Month by month me say me pay you me rent, yet yu gwaan like me don't have no argument. The bathroom is in a bad state, while the kitchen's fill with rats and roaches." Those lyrics resonated with me because I lived them. I would have welcomed a pair of shoes with a lean heel, there were times when I had no shoes at all. Michael Palmer, Half Pint, and other singers and DJs were talking about the same thing Grandmaster Flash and the Furious Five were singing about. Half Pint said it best when he sang, "the whole wide world is one big ghetto."

The sound systems in Kingston were cranked up so loud you could hear some of them from a mile away. I felt the melody of Half Pint's hit song, "we a one big family—living in a dis ya country." He went on to sing, "simplest ting is blam, blam, blam; what is this in our little island. Yes, it's all the gun fever." The violence notwithstanding, I was home in Kingston, and I was loving it. The atmosphere had an almost narcotic effect on me; I couldn't get enough. It didn't matter to me how rough the neighborhoods were where the dances were held, like Jungle, Matthews Lane, or Rockfort. Those places were not the typical spots for a Jamaican on vacation, but they were the places where the action was. I wanted to be in the thick of it, even if it meant risking my life. The threat of violence was constant, but I loved the atmosphere.

One day I was at a bus stop and two men started to argue. One man pulled out a ratchet knife and sliced the other man's face effortlessly, as if he was slicing soft butter on a hot summer day. On another occasion, I sat on a bus with an open window with a little gold chain on; I was oblivious to the thieves on the prowl in the downtown area of Kingston, waiting for an opportunity. I heard screams and when I looked around to see what the commotion was all about, I realized a thief had jumped up and tried to steal the chain from my neck through the window. I hadn't even felt when he attempted to snatch it. My attention was completely focused on the people outside, scurrying at a fast pace and hustling to make a living. These events did not deter me however, I was determined to fit back into the place where I was born—the place where my navel string was cut.

I was on vacation, but I decided to make it a lifestyle. I lived in the moment and loved it, no thought of tomorrow or the future. Money was needed to fund such a carefree life and when an opportunity came to get some fast, I jumped on it. I wasn't into the ski mask way like the stick-up kids I grew up with, but I was willing to commit other crimes to fund my new lifestyle.

GANJA MAN

When I returned to Corona, I was ready to find the kind of Jamaicans I hung out with when I was on vacation. The bus I took from Flushing to my stop at 101st and Northern Boulevard had a drop-off that was in front of a Jamaican record store. It was owned by a cool Jamaican man named Barry. His brother was a tall dreadlock who wore one of the multi-colored beaver hats which were popular among many Rastas. He and I actually had words a year or so before when my sister Nena bought a record from the store that was scratched. He didn't want to exchange the record, so I went there to sort it out. But I was in college now, and more mature. When I exited the bus, I stopped to kick it with the dread. His name was Peter, aka Peter Negus. He had lived in England for many years and was connected to a sound system called Negus Roots. "Negus" is derived from the Eritrean and northern Ethiopian Semitic root ngś, meaning "to reign."

Like many other Rastas, Peter Negus loved to smoke "sensi." I looked forward to getting off the bus so I could listen to the cool reggae vibrations flowing through the store. My college grades were evidence that I spent way more time at that record store than I should have. Peter was a feisty storyteller; I loved listening to the stories of his escapades in London, England and Rockfort, in Kingston, Jamaica. I spent many hours after school at the record store. I loved the fact that Barry and Peter were entrepreneurs who did not have to punch a clock.

I was in college, but I needed to make some money fast so I could travel to Jamaica for Spring Break. The term "Jamaica Nice," is so true. Go there once, and you want to go there twice. One of my favorite reggae singers, Junior Reid, once sang, "England nice but in the summertime, Canada nice but in the summertime, tell you that Jamaica nice all the time." I couldn't get enough of that niceness. Visiting Jamaica on a regular basis was not my only priority where income was concerned. I also had two young daughters to take care of. I had a bright classmate who was the son of a former Liberian ambassador. He managed a coffee stand in LaGuardia Airport where the Yellow Cab drivers bought their coffee, bagels, and knishes. I took a job there, but I knew selling coffee and bagels to cabbies wouldn't last long. A childhood friend we called "G Note" worked in the airport and had some coworkers who were baggage handlers. One of the coworkers discovered that certain suitcases coming in on flights from Mexico were loaded with high grade marijuana. Those baggage handlers decided to off-load the suitcases instead of loading them on the conveyor belts to be picked up by their owners. Since I was connected to some Jamaicans who either had weed spots or hustled on the corner, it was only natural that I assumed the role of broker. I made the necessary connections and the ganja flowed through that pipeline for a while until the people who were sending it on the flights found another route.

What was I to do? Decisions, decisions, decisions. The answer should have been "get a job like a normal person," but that was far from my mind. As soon as I was getting accustomed to the proceeds of my ganja brokerage business, the supply dried up. The fundamental law of economics is, you guessed it—supply and demand. There was still a demand, so I was hard-pressed to find another source. If supplying the demand meant risking life and limb, so be it. I was not deterred by the risk to my own life because I was determined to succeed with the illicit drug proceeds. Looking back, I am ashamed to say I was not even deterred by the risk to my wife and children. Back in the day there were stories of family members being killed because of a deal gone bad or when it was discovered that someone was an informant.

My mother worked hard and was excited about me finishing college, but my mind and heart were drawn to the street life. She was devastated when I left college without graduating. Looking back, it was crazy to leave school without finishing; my mind back then was far from where it is today. Since I was not thinking about nor planning for the future, I felt the time I was spending in college could be spent on more profitable pursuits. Besides, my younger sister Denise was getting tired of me coming to her the night before a term paper was due, asking her to type the paper for me. We had no Microsoft Word at the time, no spell check, or autocorrect. We had a typewriter with a ribbon and whiteout for corrections.

CRACK IS WHACK

With the advent of the eighties came the proliferation of the use of cocaine, and with that drug came a potent addictive form called crack. The mid-to-late eighties into the mid-nineties represented a dark decade for many. I was used to being around marijuana, ganja, sensi, but I don't think anyone was prepared for the effect crack cocaine would have on certain communities. No one, of course, besides the powers that conspired to decimate those communities by flooding them with the plague of crack cocaine. Prior to the proliferation of crack, the drug that ravaged the community was heroin. Crack came in the eighties, heroin decimated in the seventies. I became familiar with the term, "the dope fiend lean." It described how a person high on heroin would lean until they resembled the Leaning Tower of Pisa. Arms and legs swollen, full of sores from using dirty needles. I saw some of them going in and out of the methadone clinic that was in the hood. I'm not excusing the dude who was hustling, selling them drugs on the corner, but he was not the one bringing it in. I'll tell you what I told him, if you can't do the time, don't do the crime. But still, there should be fairness and balance in the way all people are policed, and the manner in which all offenses are adjudicated.

I was in the thick of the darkness like a thief in the night. My childhood home was located on 101st in Corona, Queens, New York City. We played football on the block there, like a lot of other blocks in the inner cities of America. During the height of the crack epidemic, one of our friends from the block was arrested and narrowly escaped the death penalty for being part of a Harlem crew that murdered and dismembered people. One of the people they killed was a girl who lived a block away from me. Her body was found encased behind a wall in an abandoned building. Ironically, the same crew was rumored to have kidnapped Whitney's husband Bobby and held him until she paid a substantial ransom.

Like so many other young Jamaican males, Peter Negus hustled sinsemilla; when the highly addictive crack cocaine hit the streets, Negus transitioned his business. By this time, the record store had closed as the crack plague swept through Corona and many other New York neighborhoods. It is very ironic that at the present time the world is dealing with a virus some consider a plague, and its name is Corona. Negus made a lot of money; he was one of the first people in the hood to own an Infiniti when that car came out. I remember the day in East Elmhurst when Haitian Jack came from Brooklyn to check on my brother and pulled up in a brand-new Infiniti. Negus also had his out that day. Two top money-makers, styling and profiling with their rides. My role models were becoming Jamaican rude boys who preferred to stab and shoot first, ask questions later. Whitney was right when she said, "crack is whack," but its use and sale caused many boys and girls in the hood to be whacked.

The intersection of 100th and Northern Boulevard became ground zero for the Jamaican crew; we were called the 100 St. Posse. After some time, we shifted to the corner of 101st. Drugs were sold, reggae music blasted out of pimped-out rides with booming speakers and high-powered amps. The music was from the fresh cassette tapes that were brought back from Jamaica. The air was permeated and saturated with the smell of high grade sinsemilla. Some Rastas still had their weed spots, but the corner was reserved for the sale of crack cocaine. I started promoting reggae parties at a local club called Club Eponi. When my friend Louie Lepke (not the Jamaican DJ) came to visit me from England, he connected me to one of my favorite DJs, Peter Metro. Club life in the late eighties and nineties was dangerous, especially if it was a reggae club. If Jamaicans were there, guns were not far. Peter Metro was deejaying, liquor and other things were being sold, everyone was feeling irie when a fight broke out. Some young guys who were making a name for themselves started acting buck wild and crazy. C Dog pulled his gun and I heard "pow pow," Leroy, who's now doing life for murder, pulled his gun and butted one of the brothers who owned the club. Needless to say, the party ended, but not my promotion of reggae shows.

PARAMOURS AND CONCUBINES

Crime doesn't pay, it costs. Crime will take you farther than you want to go, keep you longer than you want to stay, and cost you more than you want to pay. I was about to learn that difficult lesson as I moved from Bob Marley's songs of freedom to Boogie Down Productions' lyrics, "the girlies are free, but the crack cost money." I was completely caught up in the madness of that time. Years later, I ran into a former high school classmate and she recounted a story of seeing me in the streets back in the day and avoiding me because of the serious look on my face. It was a time of kill or be killed. The rap group Whodini said it right, "the freaks come out at night." I was already out when they came though, because the darkness was a good canopy to hide my illegal activity under. Drinking and hustling into the wee hours of the morning, then sleeping like a comatose person until it was time to get up and head to the front line again. I call it the front line because the government was waging a war on drugs, at any time a gunfight could have erupted.

I could trace the roots of my womanizing ways. At around the age of sixteen, I loved a friend of my sister Nena. The journey to her house was over three miles, but it seemed like three blocks. I visited her on a regular basis and spoke to her for long hours on the telephone. My mom used to have a lock on the rotary phone, but my brother would pick it. One night, I walked to her house and heard some news that broke my young heart and planted a seed of distrust toward women. She and her brother had an argument before I arrived and when I got there, he told me that my sweetheart was sleeping with the boy next door. To say I was devastated would be an understatement. She ran to her mother as I was walking out of the house, and her mother scolded and chided her brother, but the damage was done. My walk home that night seemed like it took forever. Like my dad had taught me, the spoken word could not be taken back. I can trace my later callous treatment of many women back to that episode in my life. From that point on, every relationship had to have a Plan "B." Plan "A" was polygamy, so no one would ever have the opportunity to inflict such pain and heartache on me again. The philandering fruit of polygamy would prove to be sweet to the taste but poisonously bitter to the stomach. Not only would it cause pain to me but to the women who thought they could trust me. The group N*SYNC sang,

"Just got paid, Friday night
Party hoppin,' feelin right
Booties shakin,' all around
Pump that jam, while I'm gettin' down"

Club Eponi was the Friday night spot where we went to chill and let off steam. The money and the honey were poppin', so there was no need to go party hoppin'. Gun play was quickly becoming the order of the day, that should have been a warning sign. Tenor Saw said, "life is one big road with a lot of signs, signs, and more signs, I'm gonna make up my mind to face reality all the time." In the ghetto, it is difficult to face reality because reality means day-to-day insanity. Some of it is self-created, some imposed by external forces, like companies moving factories from inner-city communities to other countries so they can improve their bottom line by getting others to stitch it, build it, or make it for pesos and yuans.

When you are caught up in this life, it seems like it's going to last forever. It was a regular Saturday night and the club was packed. Haitian Jack and some other cats were in the house. The 100 St. Posse were all there because that was our regular spot. I got into a small argument with one of the dudes from Brooklyn, and Negus got into it with another couple of the stick-up kids from Brooklyn. In the end, Negus and another dread were shot. Negus' two cousins rolled up on me in a car one day; I knew they were strapped and looking for revenge. They knew me and Negus were cool, so they stopped to talk briefly to me and left. One of the cousins was shot and killed on 105th Street over some girl. It was getting crazy, people I knew were getting shot and some were dying. There was no epiphany for me then, this was just the life I chose.

Corona, Queens had some serious cats back in the day. Bank robbers, stick-up kids and others who wouldn't think twice about killing you. I have to be honest though, people from Bed-Stuy, Brownsville, and other parts of Brooklyn might have thought Corona and other Queens folks were soft. But wherever you find Jamaicans, there will be nothing soft about them. From when I was a kid in Kingston, beef was settled with rocks, bottles, ratchet knives, ice picks, and guns.

I was in Brooklyn with a friend of mine from Corona and stopped into a bodega to buy a beer and noticed two guys walk in. I had my cargo, my rope chain and medallion on; it didn't take me long to realize they were scheming. Once I sized up the situation, I waited for the leader to make his move then broke my beer bottle and rushed him. He realized I wouldn't be a robbery victim, so he broke out. There were no more parties at Eponi, the 100 St. Posse were splintering as the rude boys looked for other cities to ply their trade. New York was on fire then. Corona dealers were being harassed by some rogue police offers who called themselves "TNT." Some hustlers went to southern states, but I chose the Midwest because I had a friend who had a connection there. At some point, I set my sights on England because of the strength of the English pound. A Jamaican bakery and restaurant opened on Northern and 101st. The hot steppers who were in town started to hang out there. Gunfights broke out regularly and the body count was rising as metropolitan cities became the murder capitals of America. Law-abiding citizens of all races were calling for lengthy prison sentences for drug dealers; some called for the death penalty. When Bill Clinton became president, he signed legislation into law which caused many black people to get really lcng prison sentences. Some deservedly so, but others received sentences which did not fit their crime. Crack was predominantly sold by Blacks and Hispanics, so their sentences were much higher than the ones Caucasians received for being caught with or selling cocaine. Racism finds a way to rear its ugly head in everything.

OFFICER OR OVERSEER

That is the question asked by rapper KRS-ONE in his song 'Sound of Da Police." In that song he rhymed;

> "Whoop-woop! That's the sound of da police! That's the sound of the beast!
> Stand clear! Don man a-talk
> You can't stand where I stand, you can't walk where I walk
> Watch out! We run New York
> Police man come, we but him out the park
> I know this for a fact, you don't like how I act
> You claim I'm sellin' crack
> But you be doin' that
> I'd rather say "see ya"
> Cause I would never be ya
> Be a officer? You wicked overseer!"

Policing in black communities was always different from the way other communities were policed; now officers had an excuse to brutalize people in the community. They were emboldened by a mayor and top brass who implemented the policy of stop-and-frisk. When the first black mayor of New York City, David Dinkins, lost to Rudy Giuliani it became open season for abuse toward the black community. One of the more severe cases of brutality at the hands of rogue cops happened when a Haitian man named Abner Louima was assaulted and sexually abused in 1997 by officers of the NYPD after he was arrested outside a Brooklyn nightclub. It was a vicious attack that the police attempted to cover up. The arresting officers beat Louima with their fists, nightsticks, and hand-held police radios in the squad car and continued the beatings at the station house. Louima was strip-searched, put in a holding cell, and sexually assaulted by the officers. According to trial testimony, one of the officers walked through the precinct holding the broken broom handle they had used to assault Louima, bragging to a police sergeant that he "took a man down tonight."[4] Years before in Los Angeles, a King named Rodney was viciously beaten by police. Although it was caught on tape for all the world to see, the officers were exonerated. And you wonder why we cry, "No Justice, No Peace." You wonder why we shout, "Black Lives Matter." Some may reply, "All Lives Matter," but when we turn on the evening news, we don't hear about unarmed white men being shot by police. There is no such thing as driving while Jewish, driving while white. But there is such a thing as driving while black. If Sandra Bland was here, she would tell you how risky that is in America.

"A fish rots from the head down," is something I read a long time ago. There is another name for it: the blue wall of silence. I will be the first to admit the difficulties of policing. It couldn't have been easy for a young white guy who grew up in a white neighborhood to have been assigned to patrol the Castle Hill or Edenwald Houses in the Bronx, the Forty Projects in South Jamaica, Queens, or Lafayette Gardens and Farragut Houses in Brooklyn. But if you sign up for a job where your motto is to protect and serve, then you have no right to brutalize and falsely accuse people in the community you are assigned to police. If you can't handle the heat, get out of the kitchen and find another line of work.

The prospect of getting fast money makes some people do things they would not normally do. There was a lot of money to be made and it was necessary to do whatever it took to keep it flowing. Guns were needed to protect the illicit trade and we certainly had enough homicidal individuals around who would use them at the drop of a dime. Snitches not only got stitches, some of them wound up in body bags. It was a crazy life, living on the proverbial razor's edge. A high-flying, adrenaline-pumping, risk-taking time. Once I was on a trip to Texas to establish a direct supply line with a hot stepper who was hiding out there. We loaded up the car trunk with the two Gs: guns and ganja. On our way back from Texas to Corona, the car started to sputter. When I looked in the rearview mirror, I saw smoke coming out of the muffler. To this day, I don't know how we weren't stopped by a state trooper. I was living what Hispanics call, "La Vida Loca."

BLOOD MONEY

Usually when a person is hit by a calamitous situation, a warning comes before the destruction. Growing up, how many times did you hear "stop hanging out with them," "stop hanging on that corner," "do not marry that person"? Check with any Jamaican and they will recount all the wise sayings they heard from their elders when they were coming up. On so many occasions I heard Moomy say, "Show me your company and I will tell you who you are; lay down with dogs and you will get up with fleas." This one I have to write in patois, "when trouble tek yu pickney shut wi fit yu." In other words, when trouble gets a hold of you, a child's garment will fit you because of the weight you lose from the stress. I had numerous warning signs flashing all around me. My mother never ceased to warn me when she got wind of what I was doing. I can hear her words clearly right now, "That's blood money and one day you will have to pay a price for it." In Jamaica when someone warns you of something that later comes to pass, we say they have, "goat mout." I don't know why a goat was chosen for that metaphor, but I knew my mother's warning was serious. If I persisted in the lifestyle I was leading, blood would be on my hands. "Out, damned spot!" is a line spoken by Lady Macbeth in Shakespeare's play, *Macbeth*. Her guilt-ridden mind was tormented to such a degree that she walked in her sleep, tortured by her complicity in the death of King Duncan at the hands of her husband Macbeth. When she sleep-walked in her chamber, she rubbed her hands together incessantly in a futile attempt to clear her conscience by washing out a perceived spot of blood. Macbeth's wife attempted to wash away the blood on her hands, but never succeeded. Similarly, Pontius Pilate's wife warned him to rid himself of the judgement of Jesus of Nazareth, "When he was set down on the judgement seat, his wife sent unto him, saying, Have thou nothing to do with this just man: for I have suffered many things this day in a dream because of Him.

"When Pilate saw that he could prevail nothing, but that rather a tumult was made, he took water, and washed his hands before the multitude, saying, I am innocent of the blood of this just person:

see ye to it. Then answered all the people, and said, His blood be on us, and on our children" (MATTHEW 27:24-25).

If only soap and water could cleanse the guilty conscience like a household cleaner. From the moment Cain killed his brother Abel, men's hands would be stained by the blood of their brothers, biological or otherwise.

The high life I chose made me feel like I had more bills than Clinton, so I had to get money the fast way. For me that meant smuggling and hustling, not what The Notorious B.I.G. called, "the ski mask way." I was living far out on the edge with no hope for tomorrow and no thoughts of the future, so Mom's words went in one ear and out the other. I knew she was right but decided I would face that day when it came. I was under no illusions that the day would not come, I had a date with destiny. I was in too deep to quit this insane game, so I only saw two choices: death, or a lengthy prison sentence.

There were great escapes which should have opened my eyes, but the darkness was so thick it would take the divine light of amazing grace to open them. One close call I experienced was on one of my smuggling adventures in Jamaica. On this particular escapade, we were aided by a local policeman. Poverty can cause people who should be on opposite sides to come together for ill-gotten gains. Underpaid, overworked policemen became co-conspirators with drug smugglers in order to make money. The love of money is the route to all evil for the good as well as the bad.

The mule I chose to use stood out like the proverbial sore thumb; in retrospect it was not a wise decision. He was over six feet tall and so pale that even the Jamaican Sun could not tan him. I was at the airport in Kingston with my partners to make sure he made it through customs and immigration. As we walked outside, we saw a sight that caused us to scramble for cover. It was Big Gene, an associate of ours, heading straight toward us, being accosted by a Red Seam Policeman. I was sure he saw us, but he either didn't or pretended not to. It was another close call, they were becoming more and more frequent. I sometimes wonder if certain things in life are unavoidable, or destined to happen? I know we have free will, but are there episodes we must go through to get to the place where we need to be in life?

During my drug dealing escapades I flew in tiny planes called crop dusters; I was unfazed by the turbulence which could cause them to suddenly drop in altitude. I had become hardened, because that turbulence was nothing compared to what I experienced as a child. While a grown man on the same plane would scream with panic, I laughed because as far as I was concerned, it was a joy ride. During most of those trips I was tipsy from alcohol, so I didn't weigh the risk nor count the cost.

I had been in several places where gunshots rang out, where people were shot and stabbed. I went on trial for possession and intent to distribute cocaine, but the jury came back with a not-guilty verdict and the angry prosecutor snarled at me, "You better watch your ass." Again, the warning signs were shining at me in bright neon colors, but I was in too deep. My life was quickly careening out of control like a car at a high speed when the brakes have failed. I wasn't hooked on any drugs like the crack addicts, but I was certainly hooked on the lifestyle, the facade of success. But that success would fade faster than a blade of grass on a hot summer's day, when there is neither dew nor rain.

CHAPTER 5

Sentenced to Destiny

THE DAY OF RECKONING CAME in November 1990. It was a turning point in my life; my date with destiny. I had been locked up before, like on one of my escapades in Jamaica. I went with a couple friends to visit their brother's place and unbeknownst to me, one of the guys who was with us had bought some ganja to smoke. Two undercover police officers trailed us back to our hotel and the next thing I knew, I was staring down the barrel of an AR-15 rifle and heard the words, "Don't move." I knew nothing about the weed but that didn't matter because the officers were determined to lock us up, especially those who were visiting from America. I already had utter disdain for the police, so this only served to reinforce my disgust. We were crowded into a prison cell in a place that I can only describe as a hell hole, paraded in front of a judge with the prosecutor accusing us of coming to the island to corrupt the locals. We played the game and paid our way out of that wretched place. Instead of heeding this warning to look for a different line of work, I went right back to my reckless and hedonistic lifestyle of fun and pleasure at any cost.

MY JOURNEY TO DIVINE DESTINY

"Three strikes and you're out" is the baseball metaphor that the criminal *in-justice* system has adopted to respond to habitual offenders. For me, three strikes meant I was in. My third encounter with incarceration would be much more challenging than the first two. The first time, I didn't stay in Rikers Island long enough to have to fight for my new Pumas. The jail in Jamaica would have been tough, but we had money to smooth things over there. But I had gone to the well one too many times and the bottom of the bucket was about to drop out. When that happened, life as I knew it would be over. I knew what the conclusion would be; prison or death, it was just a matter of which would come first.

It was November 1990, the holiday season. I was dealing with some financial pressure at the time and decided to travel to London with some cocaine. The English Pound was stronger than the U.S. Dollar, so it seemed like a sound business decision. As with my previous ventures, I never thought about being caught. My only concern was the money to be made and how I was going to spend it. I made arrangements with a contact to be picked up at the airport, and a friend who lived two doors down from me decided to join me on the trip. This friend recently told me he got involved in the game when he saw me on the corner with other players, looking like we didn't have a care in the world. Unfortunately, things aren't always what they appear to be. Once again, there were warning signs on this trip, signposts that should have stopped me. I could not find my passport when it was time to prepare for my trip across the Atlantic. When my wife found out why I wanted the passport she objected vehemently, but to no avail. I can vividly remember her telling me that God did not want me to go. I hadn't made previous decisions based on what God wanted and did not plan to do so then. I accused her of hiding the passport, and when I found it, I held it up to her face and said, "See, if God did not want me to go, I would not have found the passport." Still, she pleaded with me not to go. She asked me to think about what would happen to her and the kids if something happened to me. Every time I think about that interaction with my wife, I become overwhelmed with feelings of remorse. I can look back now, years later, and understand how concerned she was for me and for the family as a whole. There was a time when I avoided writing and speaking about it because of the guilt I felt for abandoning and exposing my family to poverty.

My life would have turned out differently if I had the care and compassion for others that I do now. My wife's pleas fell on deaf ears because my heart was callous and hardened from years of feeling victimized; I had a "my way or the highway" mentality. It didn't matter to me that "my way" was destructive. I was determined to go, and no one was going to deter me. I didn't know it at the time, but this trip would be my date with destiny.

Me and my friend Khalid drank Tanqueray gin in the cab on the way to the airport. Tanqueray was a step up from the forty-ounce Old English Malt Liquor we used to guzzle, known as a "forty" by the boys in the hood. We talked about our plans to invest the proceeds of the smuggling trip. The flight lasted about eight hours. We had some nervousness as we approached the customs agent but were able to clear that hurdle with no problem. We stood outside the airport loaded down with cocaine, waiting for our contact to pick us up; a dangerous position in any country.

MY MIND IS PLAYING TRICKS ON ME

My contact never showed, so I called a friend back in the States who connected me with to a girl he used to date. We were able to get to her apartment and unload the contraband. We went out drinking that evening and came back in the wee hours of the morning. I was upstairs in her small kitchen eating some breakfast when I heard a noise like a battering ram against the door. At first, I thought like the Geto Boys sang, "my mind's playing tricks on me." When I heard the second bang, I jumped up and started running downstairs to get the cocaine out of the suitcase because I knew it was a raid. My heart and mind raced like they were on speed; I knew it was time to pay the piper. Moomy's words about the blood money that I would pay for one day came to my mind. I could hear Paulette's words, "God does not want you to go… what's going to happen to me and the kids if something happens to you?" I managed to get the cocaine out of the suitcase and ran to the closest bathroom in an attempt to flush it. My heart was beating fast and loud, nearly in time with the battering ram that was beating against the door. The bathroom was right next to the door that the officers from Scotland Yard were attempting to break down. They breached the front door, broke down the bathroom door, and wrestled me to the floor. I had managed to flush some of the cocaine down the toilet, but they recovered a sizable portion of it.

I found out later that my contact got paranoid because he said the police were watching his house. The girlfriend of my friend lived in a known drug area and her apartment was under surveillance. Me and Khalid were taken to a police station and questioned separately. When I refused to cooperate with the officer who questioned me, he slapped me, but it was a waste of time. I told him I had no idea where the drugs came from. In retrospect, I should have copped to it because the lady of the house opened her door to us. My problem was she should have known that her house was hot and arranged for us to go to a safer spot.

We were taken to a prison in West London called Wormwood Scrubs. It was opened in 1845 and looked as ancient as it was. We were only let out of our cells for one hour of exercise and to get our food. There was no sink or toilet in the cell and there was always a cell mate going and coming. I was far from home; far from my gold chains, medallions, and silk clothing. There was no Moët champagne, no Friday and Saturday night excursions to nightclubs where hit songs from Shabba Ranks blared through the speakers. I had gotten off lightly in my previous brushes with the law, but now had a sense of the trouble I was in. From Wormwood Scrubs, we were sent to another old prison called Brixton Prison. Brixton was even older than Scrubs, opened in 1820. From Brixton, I went to a Category C prison, then to a new facility called Belmarsh. It was opened in 1991, so we were some of the first inmates to christen it. It was a modern facility; I was excited to be in a place that had a sink and a toilet. They had a computer lab there, so I went to the lab during the days and worked on the computer. The prison was pristine, but no matter how polished a prison floor is or how serene the atmosphere may seem, violence can break out at any time. Tensions are always simmering, waiting for someone to light the fuse.

One night we were out of our cells for recreation. A couple of inmates were playing pool while others were standing together talking and joking. Suddenly, I heard a commotion; when I looked in the direction it was coming from, I saw a nattily dressed black guy with a look of shock on his face and blood flowing out of his ears. when the guards came over to him and asked him what happened, he responded in English with a deep African accent, "I was just standing there, and they attacked me." In seconds a couple of inmates had attacked and pummeled him. I found out that he was accused of being a nonce, a word used in England to describe a child molester. There was no such thing among the inmates as innocent until proven guilty. If you were charged with rape or child molestation and were not in protective custody, your life was in danger. The powers that be tried to conceal what the inmates were on remand for, but in the case of child molesters some guards would inform certain inmates who act as judge, jury, and executioner. It was in the gym in Belmarsh that I received the shocking news that Negus was dead. A Jamaican from Craig Town in Kingston who I spoke with on a daily basis told me; he knew Negus and that I lived in the same neighborhood. Around the same time, I found out another friend from the 101st corner was severely burned in a house fire and died in the hospital. When Peter was killed, detectives who had bugged the pay phone in the bakery swooped in and made several arrests. Many individuals I partied and hustled with were given lengthy prison sentences and deported back to Jamaica.

I found out later that Negus had travelled from the Bronx where he lived to Corona to speak to a local businessman who owned a hardware store there, Mr. Smalls. He was married to a high school friend of my sister's. Mr. Smalls owned a multi-family building Negus wanted to purchase. Negus brought a bag of cash with him. Mr. Smalls told him he could not transact the business with cash. A contract was needed, and lawyers had to be retained. Before going back to the Bronx, Negus left the money with the owner of the bakery, then went to a local gambling spot, gambled, and drank. When he picked up the money and headed back to the Bronx, he was trailed by people who knew him. People he trusted and called his 'Bredren.' They were able to get the drop on him because he never expected the diabolical plot they planned. I believe his body was found in a Bronx park, beaten and shot. A tragic, but not uncommon event for that time and season. Negus was making a lot of money because of his connection to England. I heard there was a disagreement between him and others from the corner about the proceeds from the English business. By that time some young hungry killers were coming in from Jamaica; they wanted some of the food and would do whatever they had to in order to get some.

I've often wondered why Negus stayed in the neighborhood after so many warning signs. His brother Barry, who owned the record store where I first met him, told me that he warned Peter to leave those guys alone. As previously stated, when you are in it, you find it difficult to leave. Death, prison, or the Witness Protection Program for informers seemed to be the only ways out. I know beyond a shadow of a doubt, if not for incarceration, death would have been my fate. While in Belmarsh, I received a newspaper article from a friend about a shootout which took place on the 101st Street corner. A friend of Negus' baby-mother came across the Atlantic to do some business for him. She was sitting in his car when he got into an argument with another one of our friends. That friend was from Pain Land, the same area my brother Carol used to hang out at with some hot steppers years earlier. One of the young guns from Jamaica who was new to the block and hung around Negus pulled his gun. When the other friend saw it, he told his running partner to draw his gun; he asked if he didn't see "de bwoy back fe him gun." When the shots rang out, the mother of five from England ran out of the car in a futile attempt to escape the gunfire and was shot in the back. She succumbed to her injuries. That incident should have been the final straw for Negus to leave that area. Unfortunately, drug dealers are territorial; very few Jamaican drug dealers at that time would back down and lose face. If you were considered soft, you got no respect. Maybe Negus came with the cash money to buy Mr. Smalls' building intending to transition to legitimate business. In Jamaica we say, "you live by the sword, you die by it, you reap what you sow." Crack ruined many lives and took just as many. When my mom said it was "blood money," she was right. Don't get me wrong, Negus didn't deserve what happened to him. As we say in Jamaica, "Him neva red eye;" in other words he didn't covet other people's things. He had several children and was dating a younger girl he looked to settle down with. As I thought about it, I remembered Tenor Saw's song, "When the roll is called up yonder, I wanna be there." The roll was called for Peter Negus and Rudy Miller, may they rest in peace.

The owner of that building, Mr. Smalls, a hard-working man who owned a hardware store for many years, was later the victim of a botched home invasion in which he was murdered while in bed with his wife. The Corona posse "get mash up." I had no time to fully lament the loss. I was in an English prison with some hardened criminals, being investigated in America; my path was different at the time.

Many foreigners were in prisons in England at that time and the government was tough on people who were caught selling and smuggling drugs into the country. While on remand, I found out some people I used to roll with were arrested in the States and turned state's evidence. Things looked very bleak for me. In my mind I knew I was going to do some time, and it might be a long time so did my best to prepare my mind. Khalid beat the case and I was sentenced to eight years. He had never been in England before and it was my second trip, so they figured I was the ringleader. I accepted my fate. In a sense, it was a relief because I knew at the rate I was going it was either going to be death or a maximum sentence. As I waited for the judge to sentence me, I thought about all the unheeded warnings from the people who loved and cared for me, my friends and family. I was under no illusion that it was anyone else's fault that I was about to be sentenced to prison. I made the choice to smuggle the drugs. When remand was over, there was no going home; the time for accountability and responsibility had come. Make no mistake, I took full responsibility for the choices I made that shipwrecked my life and the lives of those connected to me. My life held great promise, but for the destructive path that I chose. As I waited, I chose not to play the blame game, to absolve myself of taking responsibility for the course of action that wreaked so much havoc.

I could have blamed the poverty I was born into in Kingston, the home environment I grew up in as a child, feeling abandoned when my mom left Jamaica and emigrated to the United States in search of a better life. I could have blamed the Black Americans who bullied me incessantly and robbed me of my meager lunch money because I spoke with a West Indian accent. I recalled being ridiculed for my lack of fashion sense, what nonsense; victimized and traumatized, for what? It was as if someone had hit the rewind button on the recording of my life choices which led me to that moment. How easy would it have been to blame the white people who chased me and called me nigger because I attended a school in their neighborhood. Because I held a job at one point in a neighborhood where blacks were not welcomed. I remember the night when it was time to go home and the elderly white guard came and told us not to go outside because a gang of white boys had told him they came to kill the niggers. He called the police and they scattered but not for long. As soon as my friend and I came out of the building and stepped onto the bus, we heard the bottles crashing against the bus windows, and saw the cars pulling up next to the bus with them hanging out the window with chains swinging as they shouted NIGGER into the night air. I could blame the lying cops who shot at me at sixteen because I ran from the home where they were called because I was throwing something at the window of the room of a girl I liked. They attempted to murder me, then lied that I pulled a knife on them in order to cover their devilish tracks. Got me arrested and placed on remand in the infamous Rikers Island Prison, where an inmate in his cell let me know as I passed by that my sneakers were his as soon as he had the opportunity.

My sentence was eight years with no parole, meaning I had to serve five years and four months before I would be considered for parole. If that wasn't bad enough, I could still be indicted back in America for things still under investigation. Did the punishment fit the crime? Was the price I had to pay right? Was it too high? I don't know, I didn't make the law, I just broke it, and the time came to pay the piper, just like Moomy said. Just or unjust, it was what it was, and I had to remember the old adage, "don't do the crime if you can't do the time."

I was sent to a Category B prison called HMP Swaleside to serve my sentence. It was on the Isle of Sheppey. When I arrived on the landing where my cell was located, I noticed something as I passed the cells of the other inmates on that landing. Most of the cells had small cards with the word "life" written on them. The eight years I received seemed like a long time until I saw the word "life." When the cell doors opened, I noticed most of the lifers were white. I didn't know what the racial dynamics were like, so I braced myself for the worst. To my surprise, the lifers were pretty cool; they went about their daily routines and didn't get into a lot of drama that other prisoners did. That was fine with me, the less drama the better, as far as I was concerned. I just needed to keep my head down and finish my time.

In the summertime, when the wind blew, there was a strong putrid smell which filled my cell. When I inquired about it, I was told there was a pig farm next door. One day one of the inmates I spoke to on a regular basis asked me if I knew what was stamped on the bags of oatmeal that came into the prison. He asked me because I ate the oatmeal for breakfast most mornings. When I told him no, he said, "pigs meal." We have a saying in Jamaica, "If it doesn't kill you, it will fatten you." I never saw a skinny pig so I guessed the oatmeal would fatten me.

As I started to make my way around the prison, I realized the quietness of my landing was an anomaly. Many of the other inmates who were doing less time were fully immersed in prison culture. They had a cheap moonshine liquor they brewed called hooch. It was in the English prison that I first heard the term, "chasing the dragon." Heroin would be placed on foil paper, heat applied to the bottom, and the person would inhale the smoke. Inmates smuggled weed, hash, and other things into the prison. There was another term that I heard for the first time and it was "bottle it," meaning the inmate would get the drugs from a visitor and smuggle it into the prison by sticking it up their rectum. The things people will do to get high and make money.

I wasn't looking to drink or smoke, so I was able to keep myself out of a lot of static. I gravitated towards the Jamaicans because that was my culture. The English called them "Yardies" and blamed them for a lot of the crime that took place. Some of the blame was undeserved because blacks from other islands and other countries spoke and acted like they were Jamaicans but when the crime was committed the Yardie got the blame. Don't get me wrong, a lot of the blame was deserved. When a Jamaican was involved in crime, they took it to the max. Some inmates had reached a place in their sentences where they were given something called home leave, which meant they were able to go home for the weekend. Home leave was not a possibility for me because I did not live in England. I encountered several inmates who were killed while on home leave or after they were released. One of them, called Toughy, got out and tried to reclaim a spot which had been taken over by some other hustlers and they killed him. I was in a class with him on remand and the next thing I knew I was reading a newspaper article with his picture describing his death by way of a shooting. Another inmate called Jinx, a young lively fellow, went out on Home Leave and was shot outside of a party.

David Somerville was a white Englishman and his codefendant and best friend was a black guy named Patrick Thomas. They had a drug case and their defense was: Patrick had a flat tire and stopped by David's house for help and got caught up in a police raid. They were slated to go to court a couple weeks after me. When I came back from trial and told them I was sentenced to eight years their countenance dropped as they spoke encouraging words to me. When David and Patrick went to court, Patrick walked and David was sentenced. Not long after, I saw David on the landing holding a newspaper article with tears in his eyes. When I asked him what happened, he said Pat was killed, murdered in his sister's apart-ment. I thought it ironic; he beat his case but lost his life. His code-fendant plead guilty and was sentenced but was still alive. Prison is not a nice place to be, but many individuals are alive today because of the prison sentence they received.

A Ghanaian inmate used to visit my cell along with some other inmates. We read and studied the Bible together. I never knew what he was in for. My philosophy was to mind my business by staying out of the business of others. One day he came to my cell sweating and speaking fast. He stuttered, so it was difficult to understand him when he spoke fast. He had a coat on even though the weather was warm. I noticed the jagged edge of a broken bottle sticking out of his pocket. When I asked him what was going on, he told me some inmates were sending threats to him. When I inquired as to who they were, he said one of them was on my landing. It was one of the lifers. My first thought was, "I didn't sign up for this." I was there to serve my time and get back to my family. I was ready to defend myself if I had to, but he was into all kinds of hustle in the prison, so I had no intention of entangling myself in his mess. I became more resolute in my thinking where he was concerned when I found out that he was catching heat because he was convicted and serving time for rape. Moomy always told me that I had to lay in the bed that I make. My bed was a prison sentence for drug smuggling, not rape. I definitely wasn't a "short eyes," the term for a pedophile among prisoners. They are considered the worst of the worst and will be killed if given a chance. Prison has its code and child molesters are not welcome or safe in General Population. They are segregated in a section called "PC" which stands for protective custody. Some people say "PC" means Punk City. A couple days later someone set his cell on fire, so the authorities transferred him. Years later I found out they cut his belly open in the prison where he was transferred.

An individual does not roll out of bed and decide to be a criminal, whether a rapist or a sadistic killer. I believe, like a seed, he can be genetically predisposed to sexual and homicidal tendencies. Once the seed is planted and takes root, it will germinate until the day arrives when he finds himself in an environment which causes it to populate. The crack epidemic caused the seed of destruction to grow until its effects wreaked havoc on the population of many cities. I certainly didn't decide to smuggle and traffic in guns and drugs in an instant. The seed of destructive behavior was planted due to exposure to a destructive environment and certain people in that environment. I don't believe in playing the victim, but I do believe in examining all the factors which contribute to an individual choosing a certain path. At the end of the day, all of us must take responsibility and there must be accountability for the decisions we make and the actions we take. With that being said, we have to get to the root of the matter so we can help people to make the right choices, or at least help them to get on the right path when they have made the wrong ones.

KEEP HOPE ALIVE

There has to be a place to keep people who are a threat to society, but there should always be an opportunity for the person to rehabilitate themselves. The debt an inmate owes to society should not be paid in toto with mass incarceration. Policies must be implemented to help offenders to re-enter society productively. It is understood that money has to be spent to lock some people up, but it must also be understood that it has to be spent in and out of prison to rehabilitate. Prisons are necessary in any civilized society. But mass incarceration because of the color of someone's skin or for profiteering is uncivilized. A person can be locked up because they are a liability to their community, but they can return as an asset if given the opportunity. Proper rehab can transform a person from a menace to a miracle. At HMP Swaleside, I made up my mind that I would leave that place better than I came in; mentally, physically and emotionally. In order to do that, I had to skillfully navigate an environment where people were always scheming, planning their next criminal move. I had to find and move with inmates who were thinking and acting positive. I had to elevate my mind and body through vigorous study, proper eating, and exercise.

The present was rough, but I had a plan for the future. Even a person doing life without parole should plan for the future. Never give up hope for a better tomorrow. A human judge may sentence you, but their words don't have to be the last where your fate is concerned. The show *In Living Color* had a segment called, "Keep Hope Alive." It was comedic but those words are profound. Keep hope alive by living today like you plan to make a great impact tomorrow. With that attitude and mindset, I was able to navigate through the minefield of madness that was prison life on many occasions. Hearing grown men scream out because the cell walls were closing in on them, attempted suicides because the craving for drugs were so great or they couldn't handle the bid, guards rushing to remove an inmate who had barricaded himself. There was never a dull moment.

"To be, or not to be, that is the question." That is the opening phrase spoken by Prince Hamlet in his famous soliloquy. After the thought-provoking question the prince went on to make this statement:

> *"Whether 'tis nobler in the mind to suffer*
> *The slings and arrows of outrageous fortune,*
> *Or to take Arms against a Sea of troubles,*
> *And by opposing end them: to die, to sleep;*
> *No more; and by a sleep, to say we end*
> *The heart-ache, and the thousand natural shocks*
> *That Flesh is heir to?"*

(Hamlet, Act 3, Scene 1)

In that particular scene, Hamlet contemplates death by suicide as he bemoans the pain of a life which can be so unforgiving. He soon realizes the alternative could be worse. As long as there is life, there is hope. Life in the flesh produces much heartache and shock, as Hamlet so aptly put it, but these things can strengthen an individual if he or she does not succumb to it. For some, suicide is the trap door through which they escape from feelings of complete despair. Human beings were designed to live so the person who contemplates taking their own life must reach a place of utter darkness where they cannot see any light shining. In such a place, it takes incredible strength to create your own light and some are overwhelmed by the pressures of their lot in life. I made up my mind to be better and not bitter. Whenever and wherever my life would end, my epithet would not read, "drug dealer, gun smuggler, philanderer, adulterer." I was going to make sure it read, "reformer."

CAGED BODY – FREED MIND

Adversity will either deform or develop a person's character. I made a conscious choice to make the most of a horrible, self-inflicted situation. In the prison system, I had two choices: elevate my mind and soul in order to become a better man or assimilate in the system and become more debauched and hedonistic than I was in the streets. I chose the former because it was not just about me, but the wife I had abandoned and the young children I had left fatherless. Left to live like bastards because I succumbed to a life of crime, unable to overcome the many obstacles I had to endure from the womb. No matter the hardships I faced and the environments I was exposed to, the choice was still mine. I could gather the fragments and attempt to piece back together a broken life, or just give in to the strife of prison life. In the streets I lived for the moment, the next pleasurable encounter. But now, the eyes of my understanding were enlightened, and I had no excuse—I had to do better or die trying.

There was no way to undo the past decisions that led to my incarceration. The choice was mine to make sound decisions from that point forward. Extremely difficult to do in a volatile, violent environment; yet not impossible when you are governed by a renewed mind as opposed to a mind addicted to sensuality and carnality. Thought precedes actions. Previous actions devoid of a disciplined thought process had led me to the prison next to the pig farm, but I refused to allow my mind and soul to be imprisoned like a pig in a sty by that kind of thinking. In Jamaica, some people are described as having a "hog heart" or a "dog heart," meaning the person had no limits to his depravity. Association breeds assimilation. I was in prison, but I refused to allow prison into me. Part of the reason I was in prison was that I became a product of the environments I was born into and lived in. I succumbed because I was young and immature, but the decisions and sentence took me far from home like the prodigal son. My heart and mind were awakened. My body was caged, but my mind was free. Instead of being in prison, it was a sentence to destiny.

THE WAR ON DRUGS

I heard slogans from politicians like, "Say no to drugs," but at the same time some of the same politicians were brokering drug deals to pay for covert operations abroad. Where is John A. Boehner, the former speaker of the House, who once stood second in line for the presidency and staunchly against legalized marijuana? I'll tell you where he is—a high-priced pitch man for the marijuana industry; making millions of dollars in an industry that he once loudly opposed. The hypocrisy is foul, it is putrid. If you are profiting off drugs, then open the prison doors and free the people you locked up for dealing it. I've never been an advocate for anything that is used to fill the lungs with smoke, simply because the lungs were designed to breath air not smoke. But with that said, I was always perturbed by the fact that it was legal to buy and smoke cigarettes which contain known carcinogens, but it was illegal to buy and smoke marijuana because it contains THC.

Black males in inner cities were given mandatory minimum sentences and life sentences under the three strikes law, while the rich and famous people the likes of Oliver North were given a slap on their wrist. I kept hearing that justice was blind but if she was, how is it that blacks have a disproportionate level of imprisonment, incarceration in the penile system in relation to their size in the American population? To say it is because they are committing more crimes than other ethnic groups is a gross over-simplification of a serious situation. From the time the Emancipation Proclamation was signed—the system was designed for it to be so. That is why Eric Garner could be choked to death in broad daylight for selling loose cigarettes. Instead of being given a ticket for this petty crime, his punishment was asphyxiation from an illegal choke hold.

A traffic stop by a white cop, may garner you a warning or a ticket but for someone who looks like me, it may result in a death sentence. The list is long; it includes male and female, young and old, weak and strong. From a grandmother like Eleanor Bumpurs, to a twelve-year-old like Tamir Rice. Because of the color of a person's skin, his life can be taken at will—we could go all the way back to Emmett Till. "Wait a minute," I hear some of you saying, "Why y'all always playing the race card?" My response to that question is something I heard a comedian say years ago, "How did the card get in the deck?"

The numbers don't add up and the numbers don't lie. The system is broken and deliberately so, because a recidivist revolving door is needed to feed the massive prison industrial complex. Now I'm hearing about an opioid crisis. When it was crack cocaine in the black membrane, the cry was "lock them up and throw away the key." When whites are overdosing on opioids it's called a crisis which needs funding, not prison. What happened to the Jeffersonian fundamental principle of democracy, "We hold these truths to be self-evident, that all men are created equal." When the Rastas had their weed spots it was police raids all day long, when the other man wanted to make money, he called it medical marijuana. Michelle Alexander said it best when she wrote *The New Jim Crow: Mass Incarceration In The Age Of Colorblindness*. We don't need traction through affirmative action—all we need is a level playing field where the constitution and the bill of rights work for everybody. I hear you loud and clear on affirmative action, but your silence on "forty acres and a mule" is deafening. How many times have I said, If I knew then what I know now—how different things could have been. How different they would have been. Community activist? Maybe—but certainly not a liability to an already ravaged community. A part of the solution should have been my contribution, not adding to a drug problem which spiraled out of control.

The War On Drugs was a ploy to continue an age-old war in America and that is the war on the black male. Freeway Ricky proved the CIA'S complicity in flooding black neighborhoods with Crack Cocaine. All dealers, myself included, were nothing but pawns in a diabolical plan to destroy black communities. Years later, we see the results of "crack babies" who grew up with mental and emotional problems. Many of them in inner cities like Chicago, using each other for target practice. My question is, where do they get the guns from? The same place their family members got the crack from. I am well aware of the asinine line from the corrupt organization called the NRA: "Guns don't kill people, people kill people." I don't believe many of these people who purport to be Second Amendment advocates do it because it's part of The Constitution or because they fear a future tyrannical government. I believe many of them believe they have to be armed to the teeth to protect themselves from some future race war. I believe some people love the idea of blacks in certain communities killing each other with guns, as far as they are concerned, it saves them the trouble of doing it themselves. I'm not a conspiracy theorist but I would not be surprised if some of these police overseers who shoot unarmed blacks were part of some secret society where their initiation rite is, they have to kill a Black person. If someone has a better explanation for the insanity, I welcome them to share it with me.

CHAPTER 6

I Heard the Voice

*"Then said they unto him, Who art thou? that we may
give an answer to them that sent us. What sayest thou
of thyself? He said, I am the voice of one crying in the
wilderness, Make straight the way of the Lord, as said the
prophet Esaias"*

—John 1:22-23 KJV

I HAVE HEARD MANY VOICES in my lifetime. Some asking
me to do good things, and some asking me to do bad things. On
March 6th, 1991, I heard the greatest voice I had ever heard in all
my life. It was the same voice that spoke to Esaias, the One quoted
by John the Baptist.

COUNT THE COST

If I had taken the time to count the cost that my actions would have,
I could have averted many of the disasters I experienced. Time
spent thinking about the impact a prison sentence would have on
my life and the lives of my wife and children may have set my life on
a different course; who knows? One of the reasons people commit

crimes is not only the benefits they plan to receive, but because they don't plan on being caught. On my way to the airport to catch a plane to England that ill-fated night, in my mind I only counted the English pounds I planned to convert to dollars when the deal was done. Nowhere in my calculations did I figure in getting caught and what that would mean for my family. I was totally self-absorbed. Sure, somewhere in the back of my mind I may have justified my actions by telling myself I needed to make the trip to help my family, but it was more about maintaining the fast life and all its trappings and amenities. The voice I was hearing at that time was my own voice; instigating, motivating, even exhorting me to stay the course. It was a course littered with explosive land mines, and I could not envision what awaited me because my sights were set on the dead presidents I planned to spend on upon my return.

There are times and seasons in life when you try to live normally in an abnormal environment. Humans are very adaptable creatures, even when their environment is not conducive to health and prosperity. I've seen movies on the Holocaust and slavery where the victims were subjected to the most inhumane treatment, yet they found a way not only to survive, but in some cases to thrive. They did their best to maintain a sense of normalcy, refusing to give their oppressors the satisfaction of robbing them of all human dignity. The slave master's objective was to rob the slave of all self-worth by reducing them to chattel, treating them as if they were animals.

THE GREAT PRETENDER

The impact of an oppressive system is not always fully understood by the oppressed. The physical chains may be removed, but the mental ones can remain for years. On plantations, black males were used to sire children who would be placed on the slave block for sale. Families were torn apart. Is there a correlation between the male slave producing children he would not be responsible for, and the problem with absentee fathers in the Black community that we see today? I believe there is. In the same manner, I believe there is a correlation between the black-on-black shootings we see in certain cities, and the self-hatred and loathing of the black skin that has permeated systems and institutions throughout the world. Once after hearing of an atrocity, I looked at my wife and asked rhetorically, what have Black people done to deserve the things perpetrated against us? Some may hear me speak or read what I write and say, "He is a racist." But I beg to differ. As opposed to a hypocrite who publicly asserts he has no hatred towards another ethnic group but makes disparaging remarks about that group in private, I prefer to boldly assert my thoughts and feelings based on some of my life's experiences. I refuse to be the person The Platters sang about in their hit song, "The Great Pretender." I would much rather be The Great *Defender*, of what we call in Jamaica, "Truth and Rights."

As a person who was socially conscious from a young age, I have never attempted to make excuses for the decisions I made and the consequences they caused. A great part of healing begins with taking responsibility for one's actions and a willingness to make restitution. I had to come to terms with the fact that my actions caused me to be a liability to my family and community; I had strayed very far from the principles of honest hard work that I was taught growing up. Instead of allowing my social consciousness to move me to positive action, I had allowed the injustices I experienced to sow anger and hatred in my heart.

I allowed myself to become one of the conduits for bringing drugs and guns to the community. I could not have imagined as a child that I would indulge in such destructive activities. I know there were forces at work in society to undermine certain communities, but at the end of the day, no one forced me to make the choices I made. I was influenced by my environment, but I could have chosen a different path. I made the choice to have children in and out of wedlock. At a young age, I knew very little about being a father and the responsibility it required. I find it interesting when some men say I have x amount of kids. They have kids all over the place that they are not caring for financially or emotionally; making them is relatively easy and can happen in a moment, but taking care of them requires years, if not a lifetime of hard work.

Someone from the neighborhood once told me he could not believe I had chosen the path of drug dealer. He was surprised because on many occasions he heard me speak out against the very things I wound up doing. It is never a good thing to point the finger of judgement at someone else because of their actions. It is better to say, "but for the grace of God, there go I." You never know how you will react to a situation until you face it. You can hypothesize, philosophize, and theorize all day long, but until you have to make certain choices, your response is unknown. You can hope and plan to take the high road yet find yourself on the low road wondering how you arrived there. Until you are tested, you don't know whether or not you will pass. The car is perfectly driven by the driver in the back seat, but the person who is responsible for pressing the gas

and the brake and keeping the vehicle from an accident under-
stands how difficult that can be.

TURN ME LOOSE NOW!

Prison opened my eyes to this realization: if and when the prison
doors opened, I could not go back to the life I lived previously. I could
not be a part of the problem which plagued my community, I had
to be a part of the solution. I became acutely aware and conscious
of my need to be the better man and not the bitter man. During my
sojourn in the English prison I had time to look over the landscape
of my life, which allowed me to see the damage and destruction I
had caused. I could not imagine going back to the status quo, business as usual. I was in need of an epiphany, though I had no idea
if it would come. I was in an environment where violence always
simmered beneath the surface, a pressure cooker where the lid
could be blown off in a moment's notice. I could simply make a vow,
a conscious decision to turn my back on illegal activity but I knew
I needed more than that. How many times have you made a New
Year's resolution to lose weight, go back to school, do something to
better yourself, only to see that resolution dissolve with the passing of time? It is good to have desire, but desire without discipline
is just a strong feeling of wishing for something to happen. Desire
has to be coupled with faith, and faith must be coupled with action.
You must believe you can achieve the change you desire, then step
out and act. The plan of action had to be conceived and nurtured
in my cerebral cortex.

TRANSFORMED BY A RENEWED MIND

I needed a mental metamorphosis. Rigorous exercise in my cell and the prison gym changed me physically, but I needed a renewal of the mind because thought precedes action. If I truly wanted to change the actions which led me to Her Majesty's Prison, then it had to begin with how I thought. The Reggae singer Al Campbell sang these lyrics in his hit song, "Turn Me Loose," "Turn me loose, turn me loose now—take these chains from off of my feet, I want to rock to the blues."

The English prison represented the chains that were on my feet because I was trapped within its walls. But the chains I really needed removed were the ones that had my mind bound to a perverse criminal lifestyle. If my mind was not freed, then the opening of the prison gates would be irrelevant. I would be like a dog returning to its vomit, a pig returning to its sty. My sentence had an expiration date and as long as I was alive that date would arrive. The mental chains were different. They had been wrapped around my mind since I was a child, influencing my thoughts and behaviors, so breaking them would not be as easy as walking through the prison gates when my release date came. Nevertheless, I was dogged in my determination.

SPIRITUAL RENAISSANCE

The awakening I needed was spiritual. I was carnal and not spiritual on the outside. The idea of a white Jesus did not sit well with me because of my feelings towards the whites who had attacked me, the ones who called me nigger! When I was growing up in Corona, I was friends with some guys who called themselves Five Percenters. Their motto was, the black man was God and the white man was the Devil. I needed a God who was greater than I was, so that philosophy didn't sit well with me. Many of the whites I came in contact with acted like devils, but I was no angel myself, far from being God. I grew up around a lot of Rastafarians who praised King Selassie as God. I respected him as a king, but I couldn't see how he was God. I understood why Rastas rejected the white Jesus in favor of an Ethiopian king who was a direct descendant of Menelik I, who was a descendant of King Solomon. I loved the cultural awareness the Rastafarian movement espoused, but I didn't see its value in terms of redeeming a lost soul for eternity. One of the things which intrigued me was the fact that they read from the same Bible as the Christians and that Bible spoke much about Jesus Christ and little to nothing about Selassie. I say little because a Rastafarian approached me in one of the English prisons when he found out I was a Christian. He had the Bible in his hand and proceeded to tell me I should praise Selassie. I asked him where Selassie's story was told or where his name was mentioned in the Bible, and he took me to a Psalm which ended with the word, "Selah." I was no theologian but thought that was quite a stretch for him to equate the word "Selah" with "Selassie." I was on a quest, a search for truth.

ARE YOU GOD?

My friend Khalid was a Five Percenter at one point, but then he converted to Islam. When we were on remand, he dressed in full Muslim regalia and always had a set of beads in his hand. When I was younger, I read how Muslim Arabs sold slaves to white Europeans, so Islam was a no-go for me. Where would my renaissance come from? There was never a time in my life when I doubted the existence of God. Agnostic maybe, but atheism made no sense to me. Dennis Emmanuel Brown, who Bob Marley called the Prince of Reggae, sang a song based on Psalm 53:1: "The fool hath said in his heart, there is no God." There are some brilliant atheist apologists, but anyone who denies the existence of God is foolish. My problem was the way people represented the being they called God through their religious practices. I took a common-sense approach to my belief in His existence.

My philosophy was, there is nothing in the world that is one-sided. I never saw something that had a top but not a bottom, never saw a night that was not followed by day. So, my thinking was if there was a natural world, and there definitely was because I lived in it, then there had to be a spiritual world as well. If there is life in the natural, there had to be life in the spiritual. As far back as I can remember, I thought the idea that this complex universe with all its life forms simply evolving from some bang was just ridiculous. An intelligent design always has a designer. The world and all that it contains had to be put together by the greatest Designer and He is God. If He did come in the form of a man, no one could convince me that it was a white man. I definitely didn't believe that I was under a curse called the curse of Ham because of the color of my skin. I remembered reading Exodus 4:6, "And the Lord said furthermore unto him, Put now thine hand into thy bosom. And he put his hand into his bosom: and when he took it out, behold, his hand was leprous as snow."

My paternal grandparents and my maternal grandmother were devout Christians. I had a lot of love and respect for them but as far as I was concerned, whites came to Africa with the Bible trying to get the Africans to live and act like Europeans. The Africans received

Christianity while the whites took control of the diamond and gold mines. They came to the shores of the land we call America and not long after, the indigenous people were slaughtered. I remembered reading the book, *Bury My Heart At Wounded Knee* by Dee Brown. The book chronicles the heartbreaking and systematic annihilation of Native American tribes across the western frontier, the same tribes who welcomed Christian pilgrims fleeing religious persecution in England. I was truly conflicted by Christianity. On the one hand I saw authenticity in the lives of my grandparents, but on the other hand I knew history. I saw the evidence of my grandparents' faith, the power of prayer through their faith, but I erred on the side of my experience.

SWEET HOUR OF PRAYER

It must have been extremely difficult for my dad to be put out of our home on his first night in America, but he landed on his feet. I believe it was because of the prayers of his father, Uncle U. While speaking to my Dad one evening, he shared with me some family history about the power of prayer when coupled with faith. His parents were devout Christians. My Dad told me that his dad woke them up at 5:00 a.m. in the morning to pray and he began by having them sing, "Sweet Hour of Prayer." They lived in an area called Bath, in the Parish of St. Thomas, in Jamaica, West Indies. My Dad was one of eight children. One morning, my Dad's older brother became frustrated when my grandfather woke him up for prayer. He told my grandfather that they prayed every morning, but he did not see any results. My grandfather told him that he would not allow him to stay in the house and corrupt the other children.

My dad was told by my grandfather that there were three countries that he wanted his children to live in: the United States, England, and Canada. He had a vision that Kingston would be the city that God would use as a platform to send his children abroad. The family was poor, but they were taught to trust in God. Not long after my grandfather's vision, one of my grandmother's cousins came to St. Thomas from Kingston and inquired where the Donaldsons lived. He was given my grandparents' address and went to the house to see them. My dad told me they had not seen this particular cousin in years. When he arrived, he told my grandparents that God spoke to him in a vision and told him to go to St. Thomas and bring my grandfather and his family to Kingston. He informed my grandfather that he had a place prepared for them to stay.

It was a great confirmation of the things the Lord spoke to my grandfather Eustace Donaldson. One of my grandfather's friends asked him how he would make it to Kingston and survive with eight children. In St. Thomas they had land, so they were able to grow their own food. My grandfather responded by telling his friend, "Anywhere you go in the world, you will always find three stones." When my dad told me that part of the story, I did not understand what he meant. In my naiveté I wondered, what do stones have to do with cooking? My wife heard me asking my dad about it and told me that in those days, the people placed their pots on three stones with the wood for the fire. My grandfather was telling his friend that wherever he went he was sure to find three stones, and he was sure God would provide the food for the pot.

Within a few months the relocation process began, and they moved from St. Thomas to an area in Kingston called Cockburn Pen.

They say eight is the number of new beginnings. Eight children were taken from St. Thomas to Kingston, then on to the United States, England, and Canada for a new beginning facilitated by the prayer of faith. In the course of time, all eight of my grandparents' children were able to emigrate from Kingston to England, the United States, and Canada. The last one to leave Jamaica was the older one who told my grandfather he did not see the reason to get up at 5:00 a.m. to pray because there were no results. My grandfather had told him that he would be dependent on the others, and so it was. My uncle had to be supported by his siblings while he was still in Jamaica and it was my dad who sent for him to live in the United States. He still lives with my dad and his wife at the time of this writing.

Every one of my grandfather's children was able to prosper in their new homeland. The least prosperous of them is the one who did not deem it necessary to rise early in the morning to pray. I told my dad that the success they enjoyed was directly attributable to my grandfather's faith and tenacity in prayer, and my father agreed.

When my dad came to live in the United States, the going was rough at first. He had to get government assistance because he could not find a job. During that time there was something called the CETA program. CETA stands for Comprehensive Employment and Training Act. My dad told me he went to the employment office every month in the hope of getting a job. The room would be packed with unemployed men seeking work. One morning he went to the woman at the desk, greeted her, and told her he needed a job. The woman informed him that she had one ticket left and she was going to give it to him. She informed him that the new president Ronald Reagan was not going to continue the CETA program. She swore my dad to secrecy about receiving the last ticket. She told him that she did not want to give the ticket to just anyone, but when she saw him the Spirit told her to give it to him. My dad was told that a letter would be sent to him, informing him of where he would work. Several weeks later my dad went back to the office and informed them that he had not received the letter. By that time, he had moved from Queens to Brooklyn. They told him they had sent the letter out several weeks prior. There are times when our blessings are tied up, but when God has something for us, it will manifest, no matter the level of the opposition.

My Dad was informed that there was a job waiting for him in the Parks department. He started working in Queens, but then his supervisor told him that he was sending him to a better park. He was transferred to a beautiful park in Douglaston, where he worked for many years with distinction. When I asked him how long he worked for the parks department, he told me, "twenty-eight years." My father received the last ticket for a job in a program that was not going to be renewed; not a co-incident but a God-incident, which was manifested through my grandfather's steadfastness in rising early in the morning to sing "Sweet Hour of Prayer" with his family. My Grandmother Edith always believed God would save all her grandchildren. With the prolific nature and potency of my grandparents' prayers, it was only a matter of time before my eyes would be opened to the reality of who the true and living God is.

OLD TIME RELIGION

Being locked in a cell for twenty-two hours a day calls for creativity in order to avoid insanity. I exercised and read all the material

I could get my hands on, but something was still missing. I found the missing piece to the puzzle of my life one day when I found a small Gideon Bible in a drawer in my cell. I had rarely read the Bible when I was free. When I did, it was the Psalms. The Rastafarians were always chanting the Psalms and my brother was a Rasta at one point, so it seemed like a good idea. I started reading the Psalms again when I was on trial, attempting to use them as a good luck charm more than anything else. It didn't matter to me that I was in court lying through my teeth. One day though, I decided to read the entire book. I started in Matthew and something happened when I arrived at John, Chapter 5, verses 39 and 40, to be exact. It was a groundbreaking, paradigm-shifting moment; the epiphany I wanted and so desperately needed.

It was a damp overcast evening, not unlike many of the previous ones I experienced in England. I had a white cell mate in the bunk above me. I was doing what I had done for several weeks, reading through the small Bible. When I read the previously mentioned chapter and verse, something different happened. I could hear, not audibly but in my inner ear—the voice of the speaker speaking directly to me in a poignant and precise manner. I had been intrigued by His words earlier in the chapter when He told some critics that He was doing the work His Father did. In my mind I thought, "What a big claim, calling God your Father." I read the words, "Search the scriptures; for in them you think you have eternal life: and they are they which testify of me. And you will not come to me, that you might have life." I was searching for something greater than myself and when I read those words, I knew I had found it. I knew I needed to have it that night. At that point I wasn't concerned about eternity,

I just knew the past and the present had been rough, and I needed a radical change going forward. I needed to get out of the hell I was in. My mind was not on the hell I heard about in fiery sermons as a child in Jamaica, I wasn't in the fire-and-brimstone hell they had preached about, but prison was hellish enough for me to want a spiritual change. Eternal damnation was not a concern for me when I reveled in sin and iniquity, it wasn't a contributing factor to my desire for change. That desire was fueled by the moral turpitude and proclivity I had to spew poison into the community for a profit. A profit that was used to fund a lifestyle of pleasure.

THE DAMASCUS ROAD

There was a stirring in my insides; I was on the cusp of getting the very thing that was missing from my life. There was a void in my soul that was darker and deeper than a black hole. I used alcohol, illicit relationships with women, and other things in a futile attempt to fill that void, to no avail. Truly an exercise in futility. Those things may have offered a temporary burst of euphoria but had no lasting positive effect. I had been on a road to perdition and I didn't care. But now, for the first time my conscience was not seared by years of drinking, drug dealing, and whoring. The words of the Christ began to pierce my sin-laden soul. I heard the genuine call to repentance; a call to turn from the filthy lifestyle which led me to the prison next to the pig farm. In the same manner that it is in a pig's nature to wallow in the sty, it is in the nature of an unregenerate human being to wallow in sin. We can attempt to cover it with a lavish lifestyle, but God Almighty is omniscient, so He peers deep beneath the veneer of respectability to see the condition of the human heart, and observes, "The heart is deceitful above all things, and desperately wicked: who can know it?" God can. How do we say it in Jamaica? "A man sees a man's face, but God knows his heart." I didn't need a stent put in, I didn't need a triple or quadruple bypass, I needed a whole new heart.

The stench from the pig farm mirrored the stench I had allowed to permeate and saturate my existence through actions taken in the street life. Like Randy Crawford sang,

> *"I play the street life because there's no place I can go*
> *Street life, it's the only life I know*
> *Street life and there's a thousand parts to play*
> *Street life until you play your life away."*

On several occasions I escaped death playing it, but now I was paying for it by playing all the way to prison.

EVERY KNEE SHALL BOW

I went down on my knees and found the scripture in the little Gideon Bible which instructed me how to repent, how to confess my sins, how to have the eternal life the speaker was speaking about. Romans 10:9 —"That if thou shalt confess with thy mouth the Lord Jesus, and shalt believe in thine heart that God hath raised him from the dead, thou shalt be saved." Before I went to prison, I could not have made that confession, because I equated Jesus with the picture of a white man with long blonde hair and I wanted no part of that. Now, I was hearing the voice of Emmanuel and I wanted the eternal life He was offering. There was no preacher preaching, no choir singing, no instruments playing, no plate in which to put an offering. It was just me and the small Bible from the society called Gideon. Someone else was in the cell but I didn't notice because His voice had my full attention.

My cell mate didn't know what was taking place. He heard me in conversation seemingly with myself so he may have thought I was crazy. Maybe he thought I was cracking, wilting under the immense pressure prison can produce. I remember him asking me what was going on, a bit freaked out. I was engrossed in the purging that was taking place inside my mind and heart. Some may call it jailhouse religion but only those who have experienced the genuine born-again experience will know what I am referring to. The words on the pages on the Bible had come alive in me in that cell on March 6th, 1991. It is a date I will never forget; it is irrevocably locked in reality for me.

THE NEW BIRTH—A REBIRTH

Humans were responsible for my first birth; my second was Divine. I started to comprehend what was meant by the statement, "to err is human, but to forgive is Divine." I was given my first birth date by my biological parents, but I was conscious of the second at its inception. The voice which spoke to me through the words in the small Bible was clear and concise. It left no room for doubt nor ambiguity and required immediate action from me. When I arose from my knees, I knew I was given a connection to The Most High God and my journey of divine freedom had begun. I was ready to face anything that would come my way, like the time I was in the prison gym working out and another inmate tried to flex by raising his voice and picking up a weight like he wanted to rush me. I stood my ground without opening my mouth and just stared him right in the eyes. My stare was so penetrating he knew there was no fear in my heart, and with the help of the guards he backed down. As a new spiritual creature, I knew I had power to overcome the works of the devil which manifested through the people he controlled. When my cell door opened, I felt an unction to share the good news of the Savior who radically transformed my life.

My conversion was not as dramatic as the conversion of Saul of Tarsus on the Damascus Road, but it was still remarkable in its own right. It had to be, because I was as stubborn and as hard-headed as they come. The Most High had to arrest me and put me in the King's Prison to prepare me for a Journey of Divine Freedom. I was too radical in my BS, my belief system, conceived to destroy and deceive through pain and suffering. Christ chose me, I didn't choose Christianity; especially the Europeanized form where the angels are lily-white and so is Christ. I preferred to mock preachers when I was drunk. "He who laughs last, laughs best," is one of the wise sayings I heard back then. God has to have a sense of humor, because He must have let out a roar of laughter when I came to myself like the prodigal son in the pig pen and called on the very name I blasphemed back then. Shakespeare said, "a rose by any other name would smell as sweet." He is, "The Rose of Sharon." Call Him Jesus Christ or Yashua ha Mesheach, just make sure you call Him. When you do, He'll answer you just like He answered me. Call His name, because according to Acts 4:12, "Neither is there salvation in any other: for there is none other name under heaven given among men, whereby we must be saved."

SOMEBODY PRAYED FOR ME

"They had me on their mind, they took their time and prayed for me" the songwriter wrote. Spiritual transformation, restoration, and reformation does not happen by chance. My transformation was no different. I firmly believe the power of God manifested through prayer was one of the keys to unlock the gate to the immoral prison which had me bound. An individual may be an upstanding citizen who never did anything worthy of a prison sentence but that does not mean they are not bound by ungodly thoughts, appetites, and actions. They may be careful not to break and violate the laws which govern the society in which they live, but every human being breaks and violates the law of God because the propensity and proclivity to sin is in all human beings. Some may believe there is no God, but none would be so foolish to say they have no sin.

In the same manner that humans share certain physical attributes, organs like a heart, liver, or kidney; all human beings share a nature which causes them to think and at times act ungodly. "Good" sinners may not sell drugs, rob people, and do other felonious acts, but they lie, think lustful thoughts, or do other things which are sinful and morally reprehensible. Lax and immoral societies can foster a culture which tell people it is ok to indulge in certain behaviors but deep in the person's heart, if they have a conscience that has not been seared by perversion and perdition, they know what they are doing is not good.

There are certain ailments for which an individual can self-medicate with some of the natural remedies like the ones my "Bush Doctor" Grandfather Eustace used on his patients, but who would attempt to self-medicate when there is an emergency situation like a heart attack, stroke, or a life-threatening gunshot wound? When the situation is critical and a threat to life, an ambulance is called. The person is taken to the emergency room so professionals can use their expertise to save the patient's life. The sinful nature is critical and will lead to death at some point. There is only one expert who can deal with it and He is the great Physician. He is the only One who can free the mind and free the soul.

As an inmate in the English prison, I was in a prison-within-a-prison because my mind was bound. Intercessory prayer was a facilitator to mental and physical freedom. My wife, my sister Janet, friends, and a prayer circle at church bombarded the heavens for me. The mantle of prayer that was on my Grandmother Edith was transferred to Janet.

An eye surgeon can remove cataracts from the human eyes which helps the patient's vision. Lasik surgery can be performed to give the patient more accurate sight. The heart surgeon can replace a defective valve in the heart, they can put a stent in the heart, operate and remove a blockage caused by atherosclerosis. We have the wisdom and the technical skills to perform heart transplants. If fallible Man can perform such surgical feats and exploits, how much more can the Immutable, Omniscient, Infallible God do? He performed the first surgical procedure when he put Adam to sleep, removed a rib and made Eve the first woman. He did it without anesthesia or a surgical team, without the expensive equipment you find in a modern operating theatre. The Omnipotent Creator of the eyes, the heart, and all parts of the body can open the spiritually blinded eyes and transplant the sin laden heart. He did it for me because, "somebody prayed for me."

Paulette attended one of the crusades held at Mount Olivet Gospel Church. The guest speaker was a Hispanic Evangelist who had served time in prison and was reborn by the power of God's Holy Spirit. He asked women in the audience who had husbands who were out of the house to come to the altar. Paulette and several women went to the altar. Paulette never met him before, but he told her I would be released from prison and I would preach the gospel. Randy Crawford and The Crusaders hit song, "Street Life," was a theme song in the streets for me, but it was at the Christian Crusade where Paulette received the word that I would be freed spiritually and physically to preach God's Holy Word. If she judged the evangelist's words by the lifestyle I lived before I went to prison, she would have said, "All things are possible, but I have to see that one to believe it." She knew how wretched I was and how I equated Christianity with the white picture of Jesus. When I came home and ministered my first sermon at Mount Olivet, titled "Don't Die in the Wilderness," she told me of the evangelist who told her I would come home and minister. When I was fully immersed in the street life, if someone had told me that I would be a Christian preaching the Word, I would have laughed. Never say never, only change is forever.

SPIRITUAL DNA

Looking back, I sense a spiritual awakening was a part of my destiny in the same way being an advocate is. I came from a rich tradition of advocates for social justice and people who were spiritually conscious. Each person has to make the choice whether or not to believe in a Creator God. I don't disrespect people for what they believe as far as religion goes. Each person has to decide which one of the world's major religions is authentic to them. I only purport to speak from my past experience of living like God did not exist, and how I have endeavored to live from the moment I became a new species, a new creature in Christ. More people have probably been killed in the name of religion than for other reasons, so I know it's not about being religious. It is about a spirituality which positively impacts not only the thoughts but the actions of a person to love and not hate. I saw that love manifested through my grandparents, in the way they loved and cared for their neighbors and gave tirelessly to help those who were suffering.

MENGELE AND ROBERT E. LEE

Although my radical Pan-Africanist mentality and the racism I experienced caused me to reject Christianity at first, I picked up a Bible and started reading it in the cell because I saw how Granny Edith Maxwell, Uncle U, and Mrs. Gladys lived as Christians. They manifested the true Christian life, not only in word but in deed. I mention the words "true Christian" because a person is not a Christian simply because it is listed on their birth certificate. If that was true, then the Klansman who burned crosses on black people's lawns and took part in lynchings, the confederate who went to war to keep the barbaric system of slavery in place; they would be Christians. The modern-day confederate who flies the flag and uses code words like "it's my culture" or "state's rights" would be a Christian. The ones who support monuments to the confederacy like the one I saw of Robert E. Lee in Charleston, South Carolina; they would be Christians. There are neo-Nazis in Germany, but is there a public park in any part of Germany where there are monuments erected for monsters like, Hitler, Himmler, and the sadistic angel of death, Josef Mengele? Jewish and other people around the world would be up in arms to protest such blatant disrespect. The black man has so little respect in America that monuments to people who fought to keep us subjugated and enslaved, people who fought to protect the right to rape our women, sell our children, and emasculate our men, stand tall in cities across America. Black people are subjected to treatment in America that no one would try in other places. In Germany it was said after World War II that some soldiers were only doing their jobs, carrying out the orders they were given. If a person is involved in a system which seeks to murder or enslave people then they have to be held responsible for their actions, whether they are a general or a foot soldier. You can't represent hate and instigate oppression and have the Spirit of Christ, no matter what you call yourself. I won't go into some of the Evangelicals who care more about the second Amendment than they care about the first Commandment.

At the moment, the church is not a monolith, yet as a group the voices of Christians have not been heard at certain crucial periods of human history. The church in Germany as a whole was silent, and in some ways complicit by not speaking out against the tyranny and wickedness of the Holocaust. When someone like Dietrich Bonhoeffer attempted to speak out, he was put to death. The church in the American South could not speak out against the atrocity called slavery because many of the "good ol' boy" slave owners were right in the church. Unfortunately even today, when rich and powerful people in governmental positions as high as the presidency of the United States make racist statements, many in the church are silent because some of the policies supported by these leaders benefit them.

It is not my job to judge who is a Christian and who is not; the words of Christ do that clearly and succinctly. Words like, "For I was an hungred, and ye gave me meat: I was thirsty, and ye gave me drink: I was a stranger, and ye took me in: Naked, and ye clothed me: I was sick, and ye visited me: I was in prison, and ye came unto me. Then shall the righteous answer him, saying, Lord, when saw we thee an hungred, and fed thee? or thirsty, and gave thee drink? When saw we thee a stranger, and took thee in? or naked, and clothed thee? Or when saw we thee sick, or in prison, and came unto thee? And the King shall answer and say unto them, Verily I say unto you, Inasmuch as ye have done it unto one of the least of these my brethren, ye have done it unto me" (MATTHEW 25:35-40).

How about these words spoken by one of His disciples who was called the apostle of love—"If a man say, I love God, and hateth his brother, he is a liar: for he that loveth not his brother whom he hath seen, how can he love God whom he hath not seen? And this commandment have we from him, That he who loveth God love his brother also" (1 JOHN 4:20-21). Even if we go by the devilish notion that a person is less than you because of the color of your skin, the Bible does not justify your enslavement, and murder of that person; on the contrary it says you should help them. That is the true essence of Christianity, and anything outside of that is a doctrine of devils.

THE LEGACY OF SPIRITUAL ADVOCACY

I feel that my purpose is to carry on the spiritual legacy of my grand-parents. I consider myself a chosen vessel of divine purpose. Christianity as it has been presented to the world in past generations has caused many critics to rise up against it, and rightfully so because of the excessive indulgence, debauchery, and war-mongering by people who called themselves Christians. For me, the Bible is the word of God. For me, Christ is the only Savior. Those firmly held beliefs do not blind me to the fact there have been many things done in the name of Jesus Christ which are reprehensible. There was a ship called Jesus of Lubeck that was used in the Atlantic slave trade between 1562 and 1568, and throughout history the church has both owned slaves and justified the enslavement of native peoples and the appropriation of their lands.

White Christians must come clean concerning the history the church has with condoning and sanctioning the enslavement of Africans. There were some Christians who did speak out against the atrocity of slavery, but racism permeated the church back then just like it contaminated other institutions. Pope John Paul II started the reconciliation process, but as far as I'm concerned reparations are still needed for the hundreds of years of free labor American and European countries received on the backs of Africans and those in the diaspora. Jamaicans are very conscious of their roots and the atrocities inflicted on African people; this consciousness is reflected in songs by Bob Marley and other reggae artists like Anthony B, who sang the song, "Fire Pon Rome."

"Black people don't get weary
Dem tek off the shackles an chain ah set dem free we
But we still under mental slavery
Unno sing with the Star Trail posse
My Lord...
Fire pon Rome
Fi Pope Paul an him scissors an comb
Black people waan go home
A Mount Zion a di righteous throne
Yogoh yoy yogoh yoy
Fire pon Rome
Fi Pope Paul an him scissors an comb
Black people waan go home
A Mount Zion a di righteous throne
Well this is my question to Issa and the one Matalon
How unno get fi own so much black people land
After dem slave, achieve nuttin' inna hand
Check out greater Portmore, Braeton
One room unno build a sell fi one million
Dem dey studio house nuh worth a hundred grand
True mi a lick out dem waa mi keep quiet
But mi a bun fire fi di one Butch Stewart
Who buy out di plane an all di pilot
True mi nuh inna Jamaica, long fi tan
Mi haffi bun fire pon the one name Azan
Everybody know how downtown a fi di poor man
How dem claims it an sey to dem it belong
No more hustling, dat mean no food inna hand
One help wi have is the Almighty One
Jamaicans help sing mi song"

In every institution you will find both good and evil, the church is no different. Anything which includes people will have both positive and negative. We have to separate the actions of man from the being who is God Almighty. I was one of the people who said, "Get out of here with that white man's religion, fools go to church on Sunday." Until my soul was pierced with the voice of spiritual authenticity. I've heard the criticism that the Bible has been tampered with for as long as I can remember. My response is if John 3:16-17 were the only words recorded in the Bible it would be good enough for me: "For God so loved the world, that he gave his only begotten Son, that whosoever believeth in him should not perish, but have everlasting life. For God sent not his Son into the world to condemn the world; but that the world through him might be saved."

It is pathetic and hypocritical for someone who makes no attempt to live by any truth found in the Bible to say it has been tampered with or certain things were taken out. The love of God which manifested in the gift of His Son for the remission of my sins so I can inherit eternal life suffices for me. It doesn't matter to me who wants to say God can't have a Son. If you can say that then you would be God because you would know what the Eternal Omnipotent God can and can't do. If you spent a lifetime you would not be able to exhaust the inexhaustible word of God. I don't have time to worry about what was taken out because my life and the lives of millions of people past and present have been wonderfully transformed by the words in the Bible. Future lives will be transformed by the timeless writings of the scriptures. This is why it is the number one selling book bar none. When you are number one there will always be usurpers who want your title, but none of them will be able to wrest that title from the Bible because it is a Living Word.

It's not the Bible that has been tampered with; it is the mind of the fool who says there is no God. It is the mind of the ignorant person who opens his mouth to make baseless assertions about the Bible; assertions not backed up with facts. Try as they may to destroy the truth by burning it, banning it, or maligning it; it will always be on top because that is the lofty place to which truth rises.

CHAPTER 7

Advocate for Truth

AS LONG AS THERE IS injustice in the world, advocates for truth will arise from all ethnic groups, all economic, political, and social strata. Without advocates for truth, this world would be consumed by greed, corruption, and all manner of evil. In every group there is someone willing to stand up to the bully; someone who is willing to be ostracized and threatened for being a whistle blower. Someone willing to put their life on the line for a just cause.

People normally advocate based on a cause that is near and dear to their hearts. There are animal rights activists who are passionate about their desire to protect animals. Some of them appear to care more about the welfare of animals than the welfare of some human beings. Advocacy not only requires having a sympathetic heart but an empathetic one, the ability to feel what someone is going through. You can sympathize with what a person is going through and not feel compelled to do anything about it. When you empathize, you are moved to action because you know how it feels. Empathy compels you to give money to a worthy cause or come out of your comfort zone to work for change. I know what it's like to be shot at and almost killed, then falsely accused of something so the cop could justify discharging his firearm; I know what it feels like to spend hours in a cell smaller than some people's closets where someone else decides when you can come out. I don't know what it's like to be on death row and for that, I certainly am glad. I would not try to imagine what it is like to be on death row for a crime you did not commit. DNA testing has caused many death row convictions to be overturned, but there are individuals who have been put to death who did not commit the crime. It may be rare but even one case is one too many. I have personal experience with certain cops, penal systems, and kangaroo courts where judges are in cahoots with wardens in prisons to funnel young black men through the system for monetary kickbacks. Systems where public defenders convince an accused person to take a plea deal so they can lighten their case logs.

I responded to the Florida Death Row inmate who saw me on Christian Television and wrote to me because his appeals had been exhausted and barring a reprieve by the governor or a miracle, he would be led to the death chamber.

I googled the man's name and found out his crime was heinous. He used his bomb-making skills to make an explosive device which he placed in a microwave, gift-wrapped, and paid someone to deliver the package to his ex-wife, who knew of a murder he had been involved with and had intimate knowledge of an active drug ring he was involved with. The driver he paid thought he was delivering drugs. He and an accomplice were pulled over by a trooper. The driver had an invalid license, so he and his accomplice were arrested, probably for having outstanding warrants. When the officer searched the car and opened the package, it exploded and

Chapter 7: Advocate for Truth

killed him. The bomb-maker was sentenced to death and was subsequently executed on February 26th, 2014. The man driving the vehicle was sentenced to 40 years. Let me state emphatically, a heinous crime indeed and probably worthy of the punishment. I'm sure every reader would agree; it is equally heinous to me when a cop becomes judge, jury, and executioner of an unarmed person who has done no wrong. It is heinous when cops who are on video murdering someone go to court and are acquitted. It is heinous when a cop buys a neo-Nazi white supremacist racist like Dylan Roof a Burger King meal after his arrest for murdering nine people in church in Charleston, South Carolina.

No person's life is more valuable than another. In this instance, I will agree with those who say, "all lives matter." All must include blue lives, black lives, and white lives. I was repulsed by the action of the person who put the bomb in the microwave, but decided to write him because I saw him as a tortured soul awaiting imminent death. In his letters, he expressed the fact he had made peace with his maker and was remorseful. The punishment has to fit the crime, but we should never lose compassion because if we do, we become as heartless as the individual who committed the heinous crime. Like any other demographic there is good and evil amongst the law enforcement community. I pray for the ones who risk their lives to do their jobs with integrity, but I must still speak out against the crooked ones who use their authority to commit and cover up crimes. A person cannot be an advocate and be fearful of speaking out.

When that white lady came ringing our bell to solicit help for the black man who was wrongfully convicted and sentenced to death row, I had empathy because I knew what it was like to be falsely accused and have to spend time in a cell. When the cop lied on me, I was only locked up at Rikers Island for hours, but any amount of time spent in a violent place like Rikers Island is terrible.

I watched an interview on YouTube of a well-known reggae artist who was asked if there was anything he would do differently, if given the opportunity to go back. He said nothing, but I can think of a plethora of things I would do differently. My reason for doing things differently would not only be due to the anguish and pain I caused myself but because of the heartache and pain my actions caused others, especially the people I love.

REPENTANCE MEANS MORE THAN SORRY

It is unfortunate when remorse is only felt after the fact; it is sad when a person only says, "I am sorry," because they were caught. A person can apologize to pacify someone they have victimized but true repentance means having a change of mind and heart, turning from the thought process and the actions which caused the hurt. "Better late than never," some may say, and that is true. Unfortunately, some damages are almost impossible to repair; some are irreconcilable. Growing up I heard the words, "coulda, shoulda, woulda." If I only knew then what I know now. I received a message recently from a younger friend and brother in Jamaica who said, "the walls were closing in." The coronavirus pandemic has wreaked havoc on his business, leaving him with a mountain of debt. His accounts were frozen by the bank. He was single, had no children and had recently become estranged from his family. I encouraged him to formulate a plan because every crisis presents an opportunity. I told him not to focus on perceived liabilities and past failures. Those things would only plunge him deeper into depression and despair. I encouraged him to be willing to apologize to those he had offended and deal with the root of his anger.

I invoked a metaphor that I use almost on a daily basis and it is the eagle's ability to rise and soar in the midst of a storm. I told him that brick and mortar can be replaced, debts can be paid off, but a human life cannot be replaced. He needed a pandemic plan and a post-pandemic plan. He admitted there were things he had not done to prepare properly, and he was going to start immediately. I remember when I felt like my cell walls were closing in. I was alone, separated from my wife, children, and other family members. It is a great blessing to have the opportunity to encourage and motivate, to advocate on behalf of another person who feels like giving up. Negative experiences, self-inflicted or otherwise can be used for our benefit if we are able to learn a valuable lesson from them. The humbling experiences I've had of being sentenced to a prison next to a pig farm taught me to be compassionate and not judgmental.

Some people who are wronged are so hurt they decide not to trust anyone. The hurt and pain I've experienced on the continuing journey called life is what motivates me to help others. Last year, when my wife and I were preparing for a series of ministerial trips to Jamaica, I sensed the voice of the Spirit telling me I was to minister not only in word but in deed. He gave me an acronym of three letters, R.A.K., which stands for "random acts of kindness." There are enough random acts of evil in this world, so kudos to the unsung heroes who do random acts of kindness without ever being recognized or rewarded. I am constantly being contacted through various modes and means of communication by people who need help. In my heart and soul, I want to help as many as I possibly can.

WHAT IS TRUTH?

When Jesus was in the Judgment Hall, accused in what was tantamount to a trial, He told Pontius Pilate, "Everyone that is of the truth heareth My voice," to which Pilate responded, "What is truth?" (JOHN 18:37-38). Before Jesus could answer him, he walked out and told Jesus' accusers, "I find no fault in Him at all." By doing so, Pilate was saying Jesus was The Truth. Truth has no fault in it. I heard this saying once, "the truth needs no crutch." Mark Twain said, "if you tell the truth, you don't have to remember anything." Jesus was the greatest advocate of truth when He lived on earth and He continues to be so seated at the Right Hand of Majesty. He is the greatest advocate of truth because He could empathize with everyone who has ever been falsely accused, everyone who has ever suffered. He said Satan was a liar and a murderer from the beginning. Men and women have killed to keep truth from being exposed.

Early in life when I was a radical advocate speaking out against the injustice of racism and police brutality, I fed my soul with the teachings of Malcom X. As I matured and the eyes of my understanding began to open, I realized how great an individual Dr. Martin Luther King Jr. was. His advocacy for truth through non-violence was truly amazing when you look at the violent vitriol unleashed against the advocates of civil rights, both in word and deed. It is easy to fight violence with violence because the natural tendency is to hit back when someone hits you. To make a conscious decision to hold your peace when you are being beaten with the batons of racist policemen, when Ku Klux Klansmen drag your family members from their homes and hang them from a tree, requires extreme discipline. As I looked deeper into the civil rights movement, I could understand why Malcolm X adopted "By any means necessary," as a motto in his advocacy for truth, in response to the extreme brutality unleashed against black people. The moral depravity of an individual or individuals who would bomb a church, killing young children, is beyond comprehension. I learned a great deal from Malcolm and Dr. King. I learned that advocacy comes from a heart of compassion and love which motivates the advocate to speak and act against injustice in all its forms. I learned that the advocate for truth has to be willing to put his or her life on the line as Malcolm and Dr. King did. In their advocacy, both men were heavily influenced by their devout religious beliefs. Being a part of The Nation Of Islam, Malcolm was more in favor of the "eye for an eye" philosophy. As a born-again Christian, Dr. King favored the principle of non-violence that Mahatma Gandhi used against the colonialist British in his native India.

When Malcolm went on a pilgrimage to Mecca and saw Muslims who were white, he came back to America and began speaking out against injustice from a human rights perspective not solely a black perspective. Prior to his pilgrimage, he espoused the Nation of Islam's philosophy that the white man is the Devil. The pilgrimage opened his eyes to the fact that there is both good and evil in all groups. My mentor Laval Belle pointed something out to me during one of our many conversations. Three of the great freedom fighters had the same two letters in their first name.

MA—Marcus

MA—Martin

MA—Malcolm

Coincidence maybe, but definitely interesting. Those men, along with another "MA," Marley, dedicated their lives to advocating for the downtrodden. As a Christian, it is expected that I model myself after my Lord and Savior Jesus Christ who was a radical revolutionary for peace and love. I am conscripted by the Love of Jesus Christ, by the great men and women of the past who were advocates for truth. Like Michael Schwerner, Andrew Goodman, and James Chaney, three young civil rights workers who were killed by a Ku Klux Klan lynch mob near Meridian, Mississippi, where they were working to register black voters.

Women like Harriet Tubman and Sojourner Truth, Angela Davis and Assata Shakur, formerly known as Joanne Chesimard. Women like my grandmother, Edith Maxwell and her daughter, my mom, Monica Maxwell. I am compelled to fight peacefully with the pen and the Christian sword, which is the word of God. Committed to see racism and police brutality eradicated, to see the injustice in the American Justice System which causes blacks to get longer sentences than other people, eradicated. As a true disciple and follower of Christ and His teachings, I cannot be afraid of upsetting the religious status quo. I probably won't go as far as going into a church, turning over a merchandise table and whipping the people who are selling stuff, but when given the platform and the opportunity to speak I will advocate for truth. I will speak truth boldly to power, whether religious or otherwise. I will tell them that Jesus

Christ and His disciples didn't spend hours in the building, singing happy songs, preaching to the choir and the converted. They went into the highways and hedges, feeding the hungry, visiting the prisoners, healing the sick. They lived and demonstrated what they taught. They were not celebrities; they were zealots committed to giving all they had to ensure people had the opportunity to pursue liberty.

What did Jesus, Malcolm, and Dr. King have in common? They advocated for truth to the point that they paid the ultimate price, martyrdom. Unlike Thomas Jefferson who wrote the words "all men are created equal," while profiting from the labor of slaves, Christ, X, and King put their money where their mouths were. They backed up their words with actions; the kind of action which speaks louder than words.

CHAPTER 8

Paulette

TO THINE OWN SELF BE TRUE

One of my favorite lines in a Shakespeare play is found in Act 1, Scene 3 of Hamlet. From the first time I read it, it resonated deep within my soul. It is from a monologue delivered by the character Polonius to his son Laertes as a token of advice, on the eve of Laertes' departure to Paris. He said,

> *"This above all: to thine own self be true,*
> *And it must follow, as the night the day*
> *Thou canst not then be false to any man,*
> *Farewell, my blessing season is in thee!"*

"To thine own self be true." I've come to the realization after many years of self-assessment that it is extremely difficult for someone to be true to others when they are not true to themselves. In the same manner, a person who does not respect themselves will not show much respect to others. I use this analogy specifically in relation to the mistreatment of my wife, which was largely based on the reckless lifestyle I lived. Long ago I heard the saying, "hurt people hurt people." It is true today as it was when I first heard it many years ago. We don't always treasure the people and things in our lives which are precious. Jesus said it best when He said, "Give not that which is holy unto the dogs, neither cast ye your pearls before swine, lest they trample them under their feet, and turn again and rend you" (MATTHEW 7:6).

"P," as my wife is affectionately known, is a pearl and I was living like a swine, like a dog. The group Baha Men was right when they asked the question, "Who Let the Dogs Out?" Some women use the term "dogs" to describe some men. In the Bible, gentiles were called "dogs," because of the ungodly lifestyle they had. Once I heard one of the guys who I ran the streets with say something that seemed funny at the time, but it was a mindset which permeated the attitude of street hustlers. He said it in the patois vernacular, "Me wife an me sweetheart affi frein." Meaning his wife or his main girlfriend had to be friends with his side chick. I at least tried to hide or keep secret the plethora of paramours and concubines I kept while I was in the streets. I must admit, I was lousy at it. I could not be true to myself or my wife because I lived a lie. His brazen statement about his wife and his sweetheart being friends would lead to another incident that was catastrophic. One of his friends' main girl told her friend who was his main girl that he had a girl on the side; when his girl found out, far from seeking friendship with his paramour she sought revenge. The incident caused contention in his home, so he decided to discipline his friend's girl who informed on him. He was no one to play with. If he even sensed someone had disrespected him, he would fly into a rage and pull out his knife. I remember one night on the corner when an addict tried to short-change him, and he pulled his knife and chased the guy. The guy ran for his life and escaped being stabbed.

I was at a house party and it was wall-to-wall dancing. I was near the door which was a good place to be in any Jamaican party back in those days. I believe it was the girl's birthday party, so food and drinks were flowing. I saw him come in with two other guys all dressed in black leather jackets. The victim was coming down the stairs and when she saw him, she knew what time it was. She turned to run up the stairs and as she did, he started shouting as he followed her up the stairs. When the smoke cleared, I went over to help a lady who was on the floor, there was a bullet hole in her leg and blood was pouring out of it. The incident wasn't a shock to me because there were rules to the game and when they were violated, a price had to be paid. Disputes were settled with knives and guns, so if you had a beef with someone you knew what to expect. You could be in a party having a good time and for the slightest infraction like stepping on someone's shoes, guns would be drawn. One night several of us went to a party in a basement in Brooklyn of all places, risky. The basement was packed, and I didn't see a back or side door; reggae music was pumping and the scantily dressed girls were wining. One of the guys who came with us from Corona started talking to a girl he saw. He is a big dude about six feet four inches tall. He fancied himself a ladies' man, but he didn't realize that lady had a man at the party. The guy pulled out a gun and started firing at him as the party goers knocked each other down to get through the only door out of that death trap. My brother was there that night and one of the bullets grazed his foot. When I got outside, I located two of the people I came with and we walked and talked about what just happened. As we were walking, we heard a siren and the next thing we knew the guy who was trying to talk to us ran right by us. He was big but he ran like an Olympic sprinter that night. One of the bullets tore through his jacket and injured his side. The siren was coming from an ambulance and he ran towards it. Just a few examples of the life I lived when I was single, and the life I kept living after I said, "I do."

MY LAWFULLY WEDDED WIFE

Paulette, the lady I call my wife for life, aka Mrs. Cutie Cutie. So many nights I stood silently weeping as I stared at you sleeping. At this very moment, thoughts of the deep hurt and pain my infidelity caused you make it difficult for me to type these words. They bring back memories of the horrible way I treated you for so many years. Dirt swept under the rug will not disappear and neither shall memories buried deep in a person's subconscious. In order to learn from the things I did wrong, I have to be willing to confront them and take responsibility for them. The lifestyle I chose to live was not conducive to being a good husband and father. Unfortunately, with so much anger and hatred In my heart, I did not have the love and maturity it took to be a dedicated husband and father, although I had the mechanism to be a baby daddy. My lifestyle was more appropriate for a person who had no plans to live long. I lived with no plan for the future, it was all just about making the next sale, finding the next club, shopping for the next top of the line outfit, and most certainly bedding the next paramour. Of course, that was like playing Russian Roulette because of the spreading of an infectious disease called HIV. One of my friends at the time said, "Live fast, die young, and make a beautiful corpse." There were many occasions during the fast life when I thought his words would come to pass.

It was a summer night, Saturday June 23rd, 1984. The memory of seeing you for the first time is etched into my heart, soul, and mind. I am reminded of the saying, "Memories don't leave like people do; they always stay with you in good times and in bad, it's just the memories that we've had." We had some good and endured some bad, but I'm so glad you never gave up on me.

I was invited by a friend to a birthday party. I was an absentee father who like so many other absentee fathers had left the raising of their child to his or her mother. I had to deal with the drama and trauma of having my mother and father leave me at a young age to live in a foreign land, and now I was subjecting my first child to the same trauma and drama: fatherlessness!

As the crooner Barry White sang, "there you were out there on the floor, the way you moved girl only made me want you more." Your hair glistened under the lights; your smile radiated like a full moon on a dark night. Hindsight is 20/20, so it is safe to say, if you knew what you found out shortly after saying "I do," you probably would have responded to my approach by saying, "no way." After the negative experience of cohabiting with and marrying a player; you would have been wise and not given me the time of day. I was well dressed, articulate, and as we say in Jamaica, "there was no tree growing in my face." I was a smooth talker, slick with a bag full of tricks. I felt compelled to introduce myself with a plan of getting your digits. I found out that your name was Paulette, but they called you "Peso." Just looking at you, even a blind man could see that your worth far exceeded a Mexican dollar. If not for my surroundings, I surely would have hollered. In speaking with you up close and personal I was irrevocably drawn to your serenity, the poise and patience you exuded. You were the antithesis of my win-at-all-costs approach.

You could not tell by looking and listening to me, but I had a lot of baggage that I hid behind good-looking clothes, sweet-smelling colognes, and the gift of gab. A facade, the charm that I used to finagle my way into the hearts of countless females, only to dash their hopes of a blissful life by running suddenly to my next victim. I looked good on the outside, but psychologically my mentality could be summed up best by Tennessee Williams' play, *The Glass Menagerie*. I chose polygamy because of the pain inflicted on me by my old sweetheart. As wild as I was, meeting and connecting with you, I knew I needed some stability in my young life and figured I needed to get married to have it. Prior to meeting you, matrimony was a word I never even considered. In getting to know you through our long phone conversations, visits, and dates, I knew you were the one. My problem was I had no plan to be monogamous, throughout the years I was used to being polygamous. Unfortunately, the honeymoon does not last forever. Once we settled down as man and wife—the cares, the vicissitudes of life, the responsibility was overwhelming.

I had the desire to be a good husband and father, but the street life had a stronghold on me which I was powerless to break. Try as I might at times, it was an exercise in futility, so I kept doing what I was doing. All the while the famous words I had heard as a boy in Jamaica played in the back of my mind like a swan song, "If you carry the bucket to the well every day, one day the bottom will drop out." It would eventually drop out, and when it did all the money, all the honeys, jewelry and fine expensive clothing could not cushion me from the meteoric fall I was destined to experience. Paulette knew exactly what she wanted out of marriage, it is what we all should want: a spouse who would love her and the children and who would work with her to build a prosperous life. When I met her, I had not dropped out of college yet. I had not started dealing drugs yet, so she was under the impression she met and married someone responsible. It wasn't long after we met that my second child Makeda was born, and it wasn't long after that my life spiraled out of control. To her credit, Paulette worked hard to hold the marriage together but as they say in the dance world, "it takes two to tango." Marriage is tough enough when both spouses are on the same page. It is extremely difficult when one spouse is pulling in the right direction and the other is pulling in the wrong direction.

Once I started hustling, the drug dealing, womanizing, and partying continued as if I was still a single man. In retrospect, my heart breaks every time I think of the disrespect I showed you when all you ever did was work hard to be a loving wife to me and an exceptional mother to our children. At the time I was emotionally incapable of being the man you needed me to be because I was laden with years of mental and emotional scarring from the trauma that was inflicted upon me as a child and all that I inflicted upon myself through poor choices. When a person's eyes are opened and they come to realize the things they did during the troubled times of their lives, they can be plagued by a sense of remorse and regret. All they can do is make sincere amends and hope and pray the victim can find it in their hearts to forgive. It is very difficult for some people to forgive themselves. In prison there was a time when I was haunted by the memories of the hurt and pain I caused.

If my prison sentence caused me to be the only casualty of the life I chose, it would not have been as terrible because I understood I had to be punished for breaking the law. The difficult part was the impact on the ones I loved. Paulette was an adult so she could fend for herself, but there were young children in our home and the two young daughters I had who were out of the house who had to endure hardship because of my situation. When I was in the streets, I had no knowledge of God's command to Adam to leave his mother and father and cleave to his wife. I had no knowledge of it because I spent very little time reading the Bible.

A man's mother and father are two of the most important people in his life, so God was telling Adam how important it was for a man to cleave to his wife. If he had to leave his mother and father that meant there should be nothing else allowed to separate him from his wife, especially not actions on his part which would cause him to go to prison or to be separated for some other reason. The relationship is supposed to be so close they were to become as one flesh. My attitude and actions were far from God's marriage command. During my sentence when I had the opportunity to read the Bible, I started to learn what God's instructions for marriage were. When I compared His instructions to the way I treated Paulette and our marriage, I knew I had failed miserably as a husband. I hear people say, "God is a God of a second chances." In marriage and in so many other areas of life, I learned that He is a God of another chance. He gives us so many chances to get it right because He is Merciful, Loving, and Kind. Paulette has the love of God in her heart and that is why she was able to stay in the marriage, praying and fasting for me until my eyes opened and my heart turned towards God.

E.T. PHONE HOME

I vividly remember the night in prison when I was able to call home for the first time. You had warned me not to take the ill-fated trip to England because it would be disastrous, but like the many other times you and my momma had warned me, the warning fell on deaf ears. I remember the harsh way I spoke to you when you told me your cousin was going to get me a job in the mail room of the company where she was employed. How I looked at you with scorn and disdain for having the audacity to suggest that a mover and shaker like myself should take a job in someone's mail room, like I was a peon. The same scorn and disdain I glared at you with when you invited me to church and I responded caustically with the words, "Get out of here with that white man's religion, fools go to church on Sundays."

Unlike E.T., it took me a long time to phone home because of all the guilt and shame I felt. I felt like a failure, a man in age but only a boy in terms of the responsibility required to care for a family. As I walked with the guard towards the office where I would make the phone call, every fiber of my being was saturated with nervousness. I wrote you many letters expressing remorse and regret for the choices I made but this would be my first call in a year. A woman you ran into in the streets told you that I had received a long sentence and probably would never get out. After speaking with you, apologizing tearfully and profusely for being a failure as a husband and father, you put our son Mario on the phone. If not for the guards in the room with me, Mario's five words would have caused me to fall to my knees sobbing. I can still hear his words ringing in my ears, emanating from the heart of a son who missed his father dearly. A father who had not been much of a father or a dad, who cared more about money than he cared about his family. When he spoke, I was shaken to my core; Mario said, "Daddy when you coming home?" Those five words spoke volumes.

His reverberating words made me realize if I was home, working even a minimum wage job, at least I could have helped Paulette with the children. There I was, in prison working for pennies an hour, instead of being in the position of a good husband and father. If I was home, I could have taken Mario and my other children to the park. I could have helped with their homework; done many other things a loving responsible parent should do. But here I was speaking to him and his mother from a borrowed prison phone, across the Atlantic as a captive of Her Majesty's Prison. I vowed that night; if and when I was released from prison, the rest of my life would be spent making forward progress. There is no way to make up for lost time, but I knew from that moment on I had to work hard on becoming a better man. It would have to start with a new mindset, a new attitude, a new way at looking at life that did not center around self-gratification. I wanted to lead a life that would make me an asset to the people connected to me and not a liability. I wanted to be a man my wife would be proud to call her husband and my children would be proud to call their father. There are many Marios and Marias out there, kids who are doing the time along with a parent convicted of a crime. Instead of justice they received a "lock 'em up and throw away the key" sentence. I was fortunate to get back home while my children were relatively young. They were fortunate because I wasn't criminally minded when I came home so I was no longer going to be an absentee father.

If someone truly loves and adores another as I have stated unequivocally here concerning Paulette, why would that individual knowingly do things which cause great hurt, harm, and danger to the person they love? All human beings have a propensity to fulfill some innate desire or craving in varying degrees. The desire to partake of the forbidden fruit is common to all humans. We all have appetites, though we like different things. You may have an insatiable appetite for one thing, but not for another. Once the individual gives in to that desire it becomes an addiction that can and will consume and destroy if it is not contained and overcome. Since everyone is connected to someone or something, there will be a collateral effect on those connected. The addict reaches a point where they are not looking for the next score because they *like* what they are doing. They are doing it because their brains crave the feeling it receives from the activity and when it does not get it, the body responds. In order to satisfy the craving, an addict will risk life and limb. They will lie, cheat, steal, and in some cases kill to get the object of their addiction. In the "Me Too" Movement, many wealthy and successful men have had their careers ruined, gone to prison, and lost their families because they were serial philanderers, pedophiles, rapists and molesters. Who would have ever thought "America's Dad," Bill Cosby would be sentenced to prison for repeatedly drugging and having his way with women? R. Kelly believed he could fly, but an unchecked perverted sexual appetite clipped his wings and grounded him in a jail. In the same manner in which the nicotine or crack-cocaine addict will indulge in highly risky behavior to satisfy their desire, a sex addict will do the same thing. A person addicted to the street life and the temporary trappings it brings will do the same thing.

In other instances, some individuals have grown up with cultural norms and behavior which make them feel as if it is all about their self-gratification, even if it means someone else will suffer. At the time I lived by Candi Staton's words, "Self-preservation is what's going on with me." I was a young heart who ran free but unchecked freedom with bad choices can lead to consequences which are dire. When I was a drug dealer, I indulged in the risky behavior associated with that life even though it was not only dangerous for me, but also for my wife and children. When I was in the thick of it, I thought very little about anyone else but myself. Did I love my wife? Yes. Did I love my children? Yes. But my actions showed that I was more committed to the streets than I was to them, as strange as that may seem. "I gotta keep it 100," healing requires honesty. I was not cognizant of the fact that love is about what you do, as much as how you feel.

A man can truly love his wife, yet he may feel an irresistible pull towards pornography and various forms of sexual perversion. The desire for the sensual, destructive satisfaction it gives him can be stronger than his willpower to cease the behavior that puts the very ones he loves at risk. The root of the desire can go back as far as his childhood. If not dealt with, it grows stronger and stronger until he is completely subservient to it. The key is to get help before you destroy yourself and do irreparable damage to your family; before you are sent to prison for years. Get help before you overdose and leave your family to pick up the pieces. Get help before they lock you up and throw away the key.

In a strange way prison was cathartic for me because it opened my eyes and made me realize my wife and children were more precious and valuable than anyone or anything the street life could offer me. I realized how selfish and self-centered my actions were, endangering the one I professed to love. I was doing the prison time physically, but Paulette was doing it with me emotionally and paid a physical price as well, because she had to take care of young children by herself. She had to deal with the challenge of being lonely even though she was married. The children had a father, but he was missing in action, so they had to spend years without me there to fulfill the role only a father can. All these thoughts flooded my mind when I had nothing but time on my hands to reflect. The more I looked within, the more acutely aware I became of how emotionally scarred I was; scarred from the things I was exposed to and the things I chose to expose myself to. Hilary Clinton said, "It takes a village to raise a child," shout out to all the single mothers out there who are akin to the whole village because they sacrifice everything to raise their children.

THE MAN IN THE MIRROR

The Honorable Marcus Mosiah Garvey said, "A man will never know himself until his back is against a wall." When that wall is part of a prison cell where you are locked in a small area for twenty-two or more hours out of the day, you have a revelation of the kind of person you are. Locked in a cell with no toilet, another inmate, and a stomach that sends you a message to get to a bathroom quickly will give you an expeditious wake up call. I awoke to the fact I was messed up emotionally. I was developed intellectually yet malnourished morally.

The healing process began for me when I did what Michael Jackson sang about. "I spoke to the man in the mirror, I asked him to change his ways." In speaking with him I had to take a look at him; not through rose colored glasses, but an honest look. I was horrified by what I saw. Years of benign neglect of the people and things which should have been important to me. I had a no-holds-barred conversation with myself. For transformation to take place, I had to be willing to confront the thought process and the actions which led me to be a felon in prison. I didn't commit adultery just because there were women around who were available. I didn't end up in prison just because I smuggled drugs. The root of the problem ran deep and went way back into my childhood. The adultery, the anger, the rage, and the prison sentence were the fruit of poisonous seeds planted many years before. Seeds that I had not dealt with, so they grew and grew until they produced fruit which not only affected me, but everyone attached to me. I was forced to take an introspective look at the habits, lifestyle, and choices which put me on the path of destruction. I faced death on multiple occasions, could have killed other human beings; I exposed my wife and my children to poverty, causing them to become a negative statistic—a black family headed by a woman who had to apply for welfare to feed her children. A family having to live in apartments infested with rats and roaches, threatened with eviction on multiple occasions because there was no money to pay the rent. In the case of Paulette and the children, the effect was great because the connection was great.

If you want to deal with the fruit, you must get to the root. You can't get victory over the snake by trying to get hold of its tail; you must deal with the head. To get to the core of the onion, you have to peel away the layers. Tears will run while you are peeling but keep going and eventually you will get to the core. Through persistence and diligence, you can kill the root of the thing which addicts you, the thing which causes your risky behavior. There are some things you will overcome, and they will be no temptation to you thereafter. There are other things that will be a struggle throughout your life but struggling with something does not mean you have to give in to it. Use wisdom. If you are a recovering heroin addict, do not hang out in a shooting gallery. If you are a recovering porn addict, stay away from porn magazines, porn websites, and other places and things which facilitate that appetite. At a relatively young age, I learned two important principles—for every cause, there is an effect, and every action has a reaction. These principles relate to things which are positive and negative. We have to be wise in the choices we make and the paths we take; the effects of our actions on those connected to us must be taken into consideration, especially if it is a family connection. As long as I was alive, my release date would arrive. I would be reunited with Paulette and all my kids, the ones we had together and the ones we brought to the marriage. I had to make sure when the time came, that I was ready to assume the role, the responsibility I had shirked. I had to learn the meaning of Polonius' words to Laertes; if I was going to be true to others and I had a desire to do so, then I had to learn to be true to myself.

CHAPTER 9

Freedom

"Freedom ain't a state like Maine or Virginia.
Freedom ain't across some county line.
Freedom is a flame tat burns within ya.
Freedom's in the state of mind."

(Shenandoah: Freedom by Donna Theodore and
Chip Ford)

THE TIME FINALLY ARRIVED, the eve of my release date. No parole was granted when I was sentenced, but prison overcrowding caused the government to change its policy and grant parole to many of the foreigners in English prisons. I anxiously awaited news of whether or not I would be granted parole and when that would take place. When I received the news that I would be paroled, I was ecstatic. When I shared it with the brothers in the group, they were happy and excited for me. The opportunity to show the world that I had turned over a new leaf was within reach and I could not wait to grab hold of it.

NO MORE CHAINS HOLDING ME

It had been three years to the day that I was first arrested. The time served was relatively short compared to the lifers I was leaving behind. Things in life are relative. One day without freedom is one day too many, but the person serving six months, one or even three years has a different outlook than the person with ten, twenty-five to life, or life without the possibility of parole. Some of the guys that I met had been in and out of the system since they were juveniles. Their response to their sentences was, "I could do that standing on my head." They had become acclimated to prison life. I made the most of the time, but I knew if the doors opened for me, I was not returning. There was too much constructive work for me to do on the outside.

A couple of the brothers had gotten transferred to other prisons, or their release date came. The ones who remained came to say goodbye. The proverbial light at the end of the tunnel had come. I thought briefly about that dark night I traveled in the black prison van on my way to my new residence. A black man in a dark van being driven to prison by a white man. The memory faded as quickly as it came because it was time to move forward. I was pretty much a model prisoner, not only because I wanted to do my time without negativity, but I understood and believed, you reap what you sow. There was already enough negativity in the prison atmosphere, and I didn't want to contribute to its stagnancy. I thanked those I had to thank for their kindness, said my goodbyes and prepared for my exit.

"All the world's a stage, and all the men and women merely players: and one man in his time plays many parts, his acts being seven ages" (As You Like It, Act II Scene VII).

The Dramatis Personae like Macbeth, Hamlet, and Romeo and Juliet in Shakespeare's plays were on a theatrical stage. I was a player in the street game called criminal life. I played many parts like "drug dealer" and "smuggler," "gunslinger" and "whoremonger." There were no red-carpet ceremonies in the street life; no Emmys, Tonys, or Academy Awards to be won. This performance was not comedic, it was tragic. The difference between the streets and Broadway was, the streets were for real, not make-believe. The time arrived when the piper was paid, the debt I owed to society was paid; it was time for the next stage. I still had many parts to play but these would be legal, not criminal; noble, not notorious. Parts like husband, father, and responsible citizen.

> *"I am free, praise the Lord I am free, no longer bound, no more chains holding me. My soul is resting, it's just a blessing, praise the Lord, hallelujah, I am free."*

> —Rev. Milton Brunson

LET FREEDOM RING

Nine times in his iconic speech, Dr. King invoked the now famous phrase, "Let freedom ring!" His words and his voice emulated a bell that was truly ringing out for freedom. Years later I would hear the words, "Free Mandela!" Jesus declared, "You shall know the truth and the truth shall make you free" (JOHN 8:32). Jesus also said, "If the Son therefore shall make you free ye shall be free indeed" (VERSE 36).

Once I received my possessions, I was turned over to the people who would take me to the airport to be deported. The van ride that brought me to the Isle Of Sheppey was in the dead of night like I was a thief in the night. But the ride to the airport was in the daylight because a new day had dawned for me; a day of freedom, of victory. Someone looking at me from the outside would not have thought I was a free man because my escorts had me handcuffed in the airport. People stared, but I had no cares because I was on my way home. For the last three years my home had been small cells, some with a cell mate. No matter how I decorated the walls with magazine pictures, I was always conscious of the fact that I was in a cell. I remember the first scripture I memorized and put on the wall,

"Be careful for nothing; but in every thing by prayer and supplication with thanksgiving let your requests be made known unto God. And the peace of God, which passeth all understanding, shall keep your hearts and minds through Christ Jesus" (PHILIPPIANS 4:6-7). The stresses of everyday prison life can cause mental deterioration, but I was at the airport in a better place mentally than I was when I was at the airport three years earlier waiting to take my flight across the Atlantic. The handcuffs could not dim my enthusiasm because I'd been free for a long time through the lessons I learned; free due to a salvation I couldn't earn. I was hungry for the knowledge of God, so I attended the Church of England services when I was an inmate. One night as I left service, the Vicar asked me when I was going home. I told him as soon as I learned the lesson I was sent there to learn, God would open the prison door. He laughed and said, "You mean when your sentence is over, don't you?" I smiled and walked away. When he said it, I was not entitled to parole which meant by law I would serve five years and four months. The law of Almighty God and timing are higher than human laws. Now I was at the airport because the lesson was learned. I didn't need to see the

Vicar before I left to tell him, "I told you so." What I told him when he asked the question is what I believed by faith, and his sarcasm could do nothing to cause cracks in my wall of faith. Being a Vicar was a job for him, being a disciple was life for me.

A white lady came over to my escorts and asked them why they had to have the handcuffs on me, they told her it was the procedure. When I entered the plane, I had a seat in first class. I stretched out and prepared for the long flight over the Atlantic. I came through immigration and customs and when I exited, my dad, wife, and brother Lenky were there to meet me. It was great to see family again. I had very few visits during my incarceration in England and that was fine with me. I wasn't too crazy about anyone visiting me in prison. The letters from my wife and the rare letter I received from a friend were good enough for me.

It's amazing how quickly kids grow. I had to learn what it took to be a good husband and father. The road ahead wasn't going to be easy, but I was ready for the challenge. Recidivism was not an option. The Most High had given me a chance to right the wrongs I had committed, and I was not going to blow it. I would always remember the prisons in which I lived, the people I met. We have a tendency to want to forget the negative experiences in life but it's a good thing to remember some of them as a motivational tool not only for current and future success but to not repeat the past. We cast memories of past failures into the sea of forgetfulness if they stagnate our forward progress. We keep the ones which represent teachable moments. As horrible as prison can be, you remember the people you meet along the way who are destiny helpers. I could not forget the destiny helpers I came in contact with. As I started the process of what the system called deportation but I called repatriation, I reflected on the way my time was spent while incarcerated and how it would be spent in freedom.

I spent a lot of my time in solitude in my cell reading voraciously. When I socialized, I kept company with a small circle of people I considered friends. That is not a word that is to be used loosely in freedom much less in a volatile and toxic environment like prison. There are some sociopaths in prison who if shown the light of a free day, they would be a menace to society. But there are other inmates who are truly remorseful for the crimes they committed; if given the chance, they would make a positive impact in society outside the prison walls.

Some of the brothers who came to my cell for Bible study had colorful names like, Sharkey and Joseph 'Pretty Boy' Green. Sharkey was an amateur boxer who ran daily to stay in shape. Joseph was the one with the sense of humor who kept everyone laughing. We were a mixed group; Carey Davidson from Oklahoma—he was young and skeptical when he joined our Bible study group, but he matured and thirty years later we are still friends. One of the best memories I have is when he came to Jacksonville with his mom to see the play based on my book, *Diamond In The Rough*. I gave him an opportunity to address the packed theatre and with tears in his eyes he recounted how his mom had only travelled on an airplane twice. The first time was when she sold some of her possessions so she could travel to England to visit him. The second was that night when she attended the play.

Dawa Hector was from one of the small Caribbean Islands. He was a tremendously gifted artist who could take a picture of you and use charcoal pencils to capture you in the full essence of the photograph. Paul Swennen was from Belgium. Meeting Paul and Carey helped me to adopt a mindset to deal with people on an individual basis based on "the content of their character" as Dr. King said so eloquently, and not on the color of their skin. Joseph Green who we called Joe, brought Paul to the meeting one night and asked me if it was okay for him to join us. At that moment, I heard the voice of the One who spoke to me on the night of March 6th,1991 out of John 5:39-40. The One who told me where my searching of the scriptures should lead. The One who spoke to me about coming to Him to have eternal life. This time He told me I had to be willing to love all people. It was at that critical moment when a human soul who had been beaten and abandoned was in need of brotherly love; he needed friends who would welcome him into their circle. It was a test of my newfound faith, a test I was determined to pass. I said sure and welcomed Paul to our group. He told us he was attacked in a previous prison and beaten with a PP9 battery. It was an assault weapon used by some inmates, it looked like a large version of a nine-volt battery. He had been accused of cooperating with the authorities. The beating was bad enough, but what really had him depressed was his girlfriend leaving him and denying him visits with his young daughter.

His sentence was seventeen years and his parents were elderly, so things looked bleak enough for him to contemplate suicide. He was so tormented he had to take sleeping medication. We encouraged him, shared the Word of God with him, and a metamorphosis took place. He started to have hope. He was able to return to Belgium where the drug laws were not as draconian. He remarried, had two more children, and was able to secure a good position with a heating company. Occasionally, he would mail me Belgian chocolate.

Having the opportunity to help another human being irrespective of the color of his skin gives credence to Luther Vandross' beautiful song, "The Power of Love." Hate is a strong and destructive emotion, but love is stronger. It has the ability to restore the most broken and fragmented life. I've never forgotten that moment, the moment I had to come to terms with the racial animus that was in my heart. Even if I felt a sense of justification for feeling that way because of unprovoked attacks, to respond to all people who had the skin color of the people who attacked me would make me no different from them. Love and forgiveness compelled me to take the high road. It delivered me from the low road of anger, a desire for vengeance. There are times when hearing of a racially motivated killing makes me angry, but I don't allow the anger to fester until it sows seeds of hatred. I am mature enough now not to allow uncontrolled emotions of bitterness to determine how I respond to what I see and hear.

All things being equal, it would be awesome if we lived in a world where skin color was not a factor of how people treated one another, but unfortunately that is not the way it is in the world. Our multi-ethnic, multi-cultural Bible study group was a microcosm on the manner in which unity can be fostered by a group of people from different backgrounds living in the same space. Black, white, or other, we shared a common experience and that experience was prison, a loss of freedom and separation from loved ones. We united around two common themes, friendship and brotherhood. I was the de facto leader of the group for Bible study because I was well-read and was used by God to go throughout the prison and gather the men for study. I was a new convert without a theology degree, but what I lacked in experience and knowledge I more than made up for in zeal. I had an insatiable appetite to learn God's word and see the lives of others transformed through His word. I remember when I was saddened by the response I received as I spoke to some of the inmates about my conversion; Joe encouraged me when he told me something his mother told him; her words helped me put things in perspective. She told him, "When someone speaks, take the meat and spit out the bones." Joe went on to tell me that my job was to plant the seed, to share the word, the increase was God's responsibility.

It was good to have some brothers of different ethnic backgrounds to kick it with on a daily basis. A brother from Pakistan who was a great cook would stop by from time to time. Brothers who did not come together to plot and scheme or reminisce about a life of crime. We came together to build one another up. We talked about the decisions we made that led us to a place of incarceration and how we planned to be different as men. It was refreshing to be in close quarters with some white men without feeling like they thought I was inferior and they were superior. I believe in giving people a chance to prove what is in their hearts without judging them based on their external look. With that said, if I get the slightest idea that someone is trying to look down on me because of the color of my skin, I will address it, but not with static and negativity. I never saw that with the group in the Bible study. Everyone was eager to learn from the Bible and learn from each other. As time went by, we realized we shared common experiences and desires like all human beings. The brothers in the group looked out for each other and made sure no one lacked the things that were needed. They came together and did something for me one year that I've never forgotten.

My birthday came and I was feeling heaviness, sadness, and melancholy from being away from home. Incarceration can take a toll on a person's mind. Most inmates have a disciplined training regimen to keep their bodies fit. Some adhere to a strict diet; I remember the first time I drank soy milk in prison, it was horrible but I drank it anyway. I was on a mission of physical and spiritual transformation. The inmates who are able to overcome the vicious environment are the ones who develop in mind, body and soul, especially through greater spiritual consciousness. It was July 22nd , which meant another birthday. On the streets there would have been drinking and celebrating, but all that revelry was a thing of the past. I looked forward to the fellowship with my brothers, but I couldn't find them, it was like they went missing. Finally, a guard came for me and brought me to a cell and when I went in, they shouted "Surprise!" The brothers had organized a birthday party for me. Food was cooked and we all had a great time. Even in the darkest places, light can shine. I greatly appreciated the fact that they took the time to get permission to do that for me. In prison, inmates have a lot of time on their hands yet still, they did not have to do that.

WE SHALL OVERCOME

When a person finds themselves in an environment that threatens their mental, emotional, and physical stability, whether they have gotten to that place through a bad decision or no fault of their own, there must be an innate desire not only to survive but to overcome. I was invited to a book signing by a friend. At the book signing is where I first met my friend, mentor, and publisher Laval Belle. The title of the person's book is, *A Five-Time Cancer Survivor*. On my way into the venue I heard the words, "not just a survivor but an overcomer." I had made up my mind not to survive but to overcome my prison experience by using what could have been a stumbling block as a stepping stone for greater. It is not a matter of if but when each of us will face a situation that seems greater than our ability to handle it. We cannot allow ourselves to be so debilitated that we resign ourselves to its ravaging effects on our mind and emotions. There must be a plan formulated not solely to survive it, but to thrive and overcome it. Survivors live to talk about it, over-comers live to teach and help others to overcome. I am reminded of the lyrics,

"We shall overcome, we shall overcome,
We shall overcome someday:
Oh, deep in my heart, I do believe,
We shall overcome someday."

The ability to overcome the roadblocks and obstacles we face every day, whether they are caused by flawed decisions or imposed upon us by external forces, begins deep in our hearts and minds. Human beings are creative and through their creativity they can and will overcome any obstacle placed before them. In order for that to happen they must adopt a "never quit, never give up, never throw in the towel" mentality. The night may seem dark, but remember it is always darkest before the dawn. The new day begins at midnight, the darkest point. The day may seem distant, it may seem far away, but never lose heart, never ever lose hope of a brighter future, a greater tomorrow. Remember the phrase, "keep hope alive." If you can keep hope alive, midnight will give way to sunrise. As a Christian I like to use the term "Sonrise."

Keep an expectation of greater; meditate on the fact that the space you currently occupy is temporary. Time is eternal and you are an eternal spiritual being, housed in a body with a soul. The temporal space you occupy is a place of learning and preparation for your next dimension, your next realm. You don't get steak-and-lobster blessings for peanut butter-and-jelly trials. The level of promotion has to be commensurate with the level of test you take and pass. You are created for greatness, so your examination has to be great. Muscles are built through resistance; the greater the resistance, the bigger the muscles. Once the muscle is built, you do another regimen of exercise to cut them, so they have what is called definition. It's easy to purchase a six pack of beer but not so easy to have a six pack of abs. The ability to rise above your circumstance must be something you mentally perceive and conceive.

My mentor Rev. Andre Cook said, "if it's not on your mind, it's not in your future." The United Negro College Fund's slogan is worth repeating, "A mind is a terrible thing to waste." My mind was being wasted when I was in the streets of New York and in other cities frequenting houses of ill-repute and dens of iniquity. It was being wasted because my thoughts were trapped in a prism of self-indulgence and getting the funds for hedonistic pleasure by any and all means. It was a prism that would cause me to be imprisoned. A mind that is not being used for creative thinking to make the world around you a better place is a mind that is being wasted. A mind consumed by avarice, perversion, a desire to get high; a mind that plots and schemes to rob and rip off other people, to get over on them, is a wasted carnal mind. Some of the brightest minds in the world are in the bodies of people who are in prison. Incarceration forced them to use their time studying books in the law library in hopes of finding a loophole, a mistake on the part of their attorney, prosecutor, or the judge that will cause their case to be revisited.

Some inmates ran large enterprises on the outside, unfortunately they were criminal enterprises. The same mental acuity, hard work, and discipline used for illicit activity could have made them millionaires in the legitimate business world if they had chosen that path. My hope is that some if not many will still have the opportunity to do so. I had a long potent and powerful conversation with Laval just the other day and he shared with me how the prison system is the new plantation. Inmates, the majority of them black, are used to work for pennies on the dollar. He told me of a situation where there was a burial for a bunch of corpses, people who had succumbed to the coronavirus. The people digging the graves were inmates. The inmate who works should be given wages which are commensurate to the wages earned by people on the outside doing the same work. Exploitation on the penal plantation is an abomination. A capitalist society always requires an exploited labor force to keep its profiteering machine well-oiled and running from the sweat of the backs of the vulnerable.

I worked out in my cell and went to the gym when I was locked up in England, but I spent just as much time reading and studying my favorite book, the Bible. When I was at Belmarsh, I visited the computer lab and practiced typing. I started teaching myself Spanish. If my time was longer (and I'm glad it wasn't) I would have worked on getting a theology degree. I was training myself mentally and physically in prison, a place I call the belly of the beast, to be a better man inside and most certainly when I got out. I had no clue at the time that I would get a job at a mortgage company where I would meet someone who had just written her first book. Intrigued by her authorship, I told her I would like to write a book one day and she responded, "Fidel, I'll help you." She gave me the blueprint for starting and getting my book published. When she did, I realized The Most High had me going to the computer lab at HMP Belmarsh to practice typing, not because I was bored, but because one day I would write my story. That day came in 2007 when I typed and published the manuscript for my first book, *Mercy And The Sufficiency Of Grace*. When I was at the keyboard in Belmarsh typing, I wondered at times why I was doing it, since I thought typing was for secretaries or for people who worked for newspapers. After all, when I had typing class in junior high, I took it for a joke. You have to see purpose in the positive things you do, even if they seem insignificant at the time.

There is a cause to every effect, a reaction to every action, whether for good or evil. You may have the desire to do something at one point that will lead to something greater later on. You have to be sensitive and discerning about which activities will have a greater value for your life and the people connected to you. When I published my book, *Diamond In The Rough*, the idea came to me to have a play written with the same title. I mentioned earlier that Carey from the Swaleside Bible study came with his mom from

Oklahoma to see that play. I was able to have it premiered at the Ritz Theatre here in Jacksonville, Florida, and the performance was sold out. When I was first arrested in England and faced a lengthy sentence not only there but also in America, things looked bleak at the time. Through diligence and perseverance, I positioned myself to be better and to do greater. Thought has to precede action. The action can only be positive if the thoughts are positive. Think small and you will act and live small. Thinking is free, so why not think big. Faith is free, so why not have the faith to believe you are destined for greater. A prison cell, a sick body, other things which are confining can cage you physically, but they should never be allowed to cage you mentally. Several of the Apostle Paul's letters are called, "Prison Epistles." These refer to four letters written by the Apostle Paul while he was under house arrest in Rome. Each letter—Ephesians, Philippians, Colossians, and Philemon—is addressed to a specific church or, in the case of Philemon, an individual. Paul penned each epistle to address specific needs of first-century Christians and the church, but the message of the Prison Epistles continues to impact lives today.

LAZARUS, COME FORTH

Every one of us has the potential to greatly impact the world. The question is, do we have the discipline to make a difference? You may never reach the pinnacle like a person who is elected president, but you still have the potential to be great. Achieving greatness is not easy; if it was, it would be achieved by many. There is a reason why a diamond is a diamond and a cubic zirconia is not, they go through a different process to become what they are. Greatness requires a process, mediocrity does not. The few achieve it because they are dedicated, have a relentless work ethic, and a mentality which drives them to succeed. The majority are willing to settle for being average. You cannot and should not be faulted in life if you don't achieve something great, you should be faulted if you are unwilling to try. It is better to try and fail than to have not tried at all because in the larger scheme of things it was not a failure but a teachable moment. It is all a matter of perspective, how you look at the situation. Let me give you a Biblical example. When Jesus' friend Lazarus died and Jesus came to the place where they had placed his body, there were mourners there weeping and wailing. Their outlook was different from Jesus' outlook; they saw a situation that was gory while Jesus saw an opportunity to manifest glory. They came to a burial, but Jesus came to a resurrection. How do you see and perceive your situation? Do you see it as dead, or do you see it as an opportunity for a resurrection? Do you see it as a failure, or do you see it as a teachable moment? Positive perspective will transform your environment. Since association breeds assimilation, make sure the people in your sphere of influence have the mindset to overcome obstacles and achieve greatness.

We have different skill sets but all of us have a set of skills. Our proficiency levels are different but all of us can be proficient in something. Our skill sets and proficiency should be an asset to our community and not a liability. If you love drugs, don't become a dealer or an addict; become a pharmacist, get a license to grow and distribute medical marijuana. Some are thinkers, some are tinkers. Whether you work with your brain or your hands, do it with excellence. Do it in a manner that will cause people to pause and say, "That is awesome." What is the difference between us? Some of us refuse to settle for mediocrity. We consider ourselves eagles. The greater the storm, the higher we soar. Teaching through the mediums of speaking and writing are two of the things I am passionate about. An interesting combination for sure when you consider the fact that speaking with a Jamaican accent caused me to be picked on. In junior high, I was placed in an English as a Second Language course, now I am paid for writing and speaking. It is what I do for a living. You know you are doing what you love when you are willing to do it for free. Portions of the prison sentence caused misery but through perseverance the misery has given way to ministry, the ability to help others through service.

My writing can encourage a brother or sister dealing with the pressures of incarceration to know that if I can do it, so can they. They can write and publish a book; they can do something meaningful that changes the lives of others. The modicum of success I've gained since I've been home through re-inventing myself did not come easy. It came through tenacity and hard work, an unrelenting will to use my gifts to help and advocate for others. When I get the vibe to write a manuscript, my focus becomes ferocious. After my morning prayer and meditation, I hit the keypad and let my fingers do the typing, maybe for you it means picking up pen and paper and writing that play, that rhyme, your memoir, your autobiography. Once I start, I type for 6 to 8 hours, refusing to allow distractions to cut into my writing time.

You would be amazed at the level of greatness which is within you if you are willing to take the time to cultivate and develop yourself. I have the stage play for my book and now it is time to go to the next dimension by having one of them adapted into a screenplay for a movie or a documentary. God willing, it's in my future because it is in my mind. If you can think it, you can achieve it. The sky is not the limit, as a spiritual being you have no limit.

Once you allow greatness to come forth, you will be amazed the impact it has on others. I was home one Sunday morning in meditation, looking out my bedroom window when I saw a call coming in from an unlisted number. I normally let those calls go to voicemail, but I decided to answer this one. It was from someone who was recently released from a federal prison and was now living in a half-way house. He told me how my book, *From The Pit To The Prison To The Palace*, helped him while he was inside. He told me he planned to find a job so he could get his own apartment. He also told me he desired to write a book one day and I let him know I would help him. I was a prisoner once, I came out and found a job, and someone on that job helped me write the first of many books. I believe in paying kindness forward; blessed not to be selfish but to be selfless, blessed to be a blessing to others.

I was on a ministry assignment in Norfolk, Virginia and a lady came to my table and told me her boss had a son who was in prison. She picked up my book, *From The Pit* and said she wanted to purchase it in order to send it to him. I told her I wanted to give it to him as a gift. Several months later I received a call from an unlisted number and when I listened to the voicemail it was from a man in Virginia who asked if I could give him a call. He turned out to be the son of the lady's boss. He was out of prison and told me how the book blessed him when he was locked up. He was very emotional as he spoke with me. He told me he had thought about calling me on several occasions, but he was waiting for the right time. He had some technical skills and said he wanted to use those skills along with what he learned from the Bible to teach young people. One of my greatest joys is the letters, phone calls, and messages I receive from inmates about how one of my books have blessed, motivated, and inspired them. To know that the words I have been inspired to write is a source of inspiration and motivation is very redemptive for me. It is part and parcel of what makes advocacy so important for me.

"An idle mind is the devil's playground" was something I heard many times. Coming home, I knew I had no time for idleness. Having been away from family meant there was much work to be done, not to mention the work that needed to be done to make a living. I didn't really know where I *would* start but I knew I would start. Diana Ross' song had the hook,

> *"I'm coming out*
> *I want the world to know*
> *Got to let it show*
> *I'm coming out*
> *I want the world to know*
> *I got to let it show."*

Before I went in, the world saw my bling, they peeped my gold necklace and my gold ring. Back then I showed them style, but now I was determined to show them substance. No more wild child from the streets, but a child of God determined to preach Good News.

My friend Gilbert Purdie encouraged me to finish the work to get my college degree. I must have been really out there mentally and emotionally when I dropped out of college for the streets. I know because when I went to Queens College to find out how many semesters I would need to take to get my degree, I found out that I was only three credits shy of graduating. I met with a cool Ghanaian professor of African Studies by the name of Ofuatey Kodjoe. (It has been many years since so please forgive me if I spelled his name wrong!) He assigned me to write a paper and upon completion of the paper I was able to receive a Bachelor's Degree in Political Science. It was a watershed moment for me because it was indicative of a positive new start. The blow of the stigma of being an ex-convict was softened because I had achieved something not many achieved, I had received my college degree. That degree would help greatly when it was time to interview for a job. I wasn't full of pride like I was back in the day when I berated my wife for suggesting I take a job in the mail room. My mom taught me when I was younger that I couldn't eat pride. Pride can't pay bills and it can't take care of your kids, so I was willing to do what was necessary and legal to help my family.

WHEN THE GOING GETS TOUGH

The going was rough in the beginning. One day my son Mario looked me in the eyes and said, "Daddy we're poor." When I was locked up it was, "Daddy when you coming home?" but now that I was home, it was "Daddy, we're poor." Kids say the darnedest things.

It is very humbling as a man when your son looks at you and speaks honestly like children do about a situation. Fathers are providers, they are supposed to be strong. My son realized he didn't have the things other kids in school and in the neighborhood had.

178

An apartment overrun by rats and roaches also made him realize we were poor. He did what every son should be able to do, he spoke to his dad. Unfortunately, at the time his dad was dealing with an impoverished situation created by decisions made years before. I was challenged but doing what I previously did was not an option. Getting a package and hitting the corner or opening up a spot was out of the question. I wasn't going to do anything to exacerbate an already serious situation. Crime was not an option. My wife and kids would not be put in a situation again where they would be a statistic. My brother Lenky gave me some cash and I went to Delaney Street where I bought my clothes years before and bought some clothes wholesale and started selling them. I wound up giving a lot of them away on credit and never collected the money, so my wife told me it didn't make sense.

Eventually I was able to get a temp job in the fax department at Goldman Sachs, which allowed me to sit near and overhear some of the brightest business minds in America. The analysts, associates, vice presidents, and partners had graduated from some of the top business schools in the country. One of the things I noticed about them was how driven they were to succeed. They worked long hours to close deals. Watching and listening to them made me realize what it would take to be successful. One day I was in the elevator with John Corzine and Henry 'Hank' Paulson. They were the president and vice president of the company at the time. John Corzine would go on to be the Governor of New Jersey and Hank Paulson became Secretary of the U.S. Treasury when George W. Bush was president. I wound up leaving that position because they started doing background checks. Although my criminal past was in England, I didn't want to lie so I quit. I left there with confidence. Working around some of the brightest business minds gave me a lot of confidence. When one door is closed, another will open. I was ready for the next door, and it came with a permanent job at Channel Thirteen. I didn't want to lie on the application about my background because the application asked if I have been convicted of a crime in the last seven years. At the time I was past the seven-year mark of my arrest and conviction in England.

I was so thankful for the opportunity to have permanent employment and help my family that I made sure I was a model employee. I went to work on time, did what I was asked, and worked very hard. I was Black and West Indian in a predominantly white environment, so I made sure I represented myself well. A few years later when it was time to relocate to Florida, the manager of the department asked me if I was sure and I told her yes. She said something which blessed me, "Your chair will always be here." Her words gave me further confidence that I could excel in a work environment. I could not afford a car at the time like many of the people I worked with or came in contact with, but I didn't complain because I had a JOB.

SPIRITUAL NOT CARNAL

Prison was the place where I received spiritual awareness and consciousness. I was determined to grow strong in my faith, stronger in my walk. I had an encounter with The Most High in prison and would not settle for anything fake. On the outside I realized that it was of the utmost importance for me to be spiritually connected. I had read the Bible and lived long enough to know that the old nature, referred to as the carnal nature in the Bible, was always looking for an opportunity to regain control. I remembered Jesus' words, "When the unclean spirit is gone out of a man, he walketh through dry places, seeking rest, and findeth none. Then he saith, I will return into my house from whence I came out; and when he is come, he findeth it empty, swept, and garnished. Then goeth he, and taketh with himself seven other spirits more wicked than himself, and they enter in and dwell there: and the last state of that man is worse than the first. Even so shall it be also unto this wicked generation." (MATTHEW 12:43-45). If I was going to grow spiritually, I needed to be planted.

THE BLESSED MAN

No man is an island, meaning every man is going to need someone to help them at some point. I read and studied the scriptures voraciously, but I knew I still needed to be taught, not to mention the fact I needed fellowship to grow. The Bible speaks about desiring the sincerest milk of the word. In the same manner that natural babies use milk to grow and strengthen their bones, newborn spiritual babies need the milk of God's Word. I wanted of the all blessings I read about in the scriptures. I wanted to be like the person I call "The Psalm 1 Man,"

> *"His delight is in the law of the Lord; and in his law doth he meditate day and night. And he shall be like a tree planted by the rivers of water, that bringeth forth his fruit in his season; his leaf also shall not wither; and whatsoever he doeth shall prosper" (PSALMS 1:2-3).*

I needed to be around men who loved God and manifested that love in the way they treated their wives, children, and others. Prior to prison I had spent years around hustling men who loved guns and the trappings the street life brought. A great deal is told by the company we keep, so I wanted some Kingdom Company, not necessarily Church Company. There are people who are in Church but keep up a lot of the mess they kept up in the world. I had studied enough to know how Kingdom People behaved, and that was much different from Church People. At the time, my wife and children attended the same church I attended when I was a child, Mount Olivet Gospel Church in Corona, Queens. They had a solid men's group led by then Deacon Stuart Sid Barrett. I attended Saturday men's meeting and learned all I could from the strong men of God who attended the meeting. I started growing spiritually because I maintained the same voracious appetite for the word of God that I had when I was in prison. When I was locked up, I wrote many letters to Paulette with questions about what I read. She shared with me what she knew in her letters and what she did not know she asked people who did so she could give me the answers I needed. A deacon by the name of Elder Marvin Ruff took me under his wing and allowed me to attend the church outreach at Elmcor, a drug and alcohol rehabilitation center. I looked forward to attending because years earlier I was selling rocks to crack heads in the neighborhood but now I was giving them knowledge about the Rock Of Ages and how he had transformed my life. I felt honored to have the opportunity to minister to individuals who were suffering because of decisions they made to use drugs. I had suffered because of the decision I made to sell drugs. When I saw those souls, I saw the collateral damage done to the lives of other human beings by the drug trade. At the end of the day, each human being is responsible for the decisions they make, the actions they undertake; but it is not a good thing when you are the supplier of the poison that they use to destroy themselves. Those who know better should not only do better, they should help others to do the same. When Cain was caught, instead of confessing he asked the question, "Am I my brother's keeper?" the answer must be a resounding, "Yes, you are!"

The team from Mount Olivet went to Elmcor once a month. I looked forward to those Sundays because they represented what Jesus told His disciples in The Great Commission; He told them to go and teach and make disciples. The Lord spoke to my heart on one of our meetings at Elmcor about the need to be there more than once per month. I realized that the residents needed an ongoing time of teaching and fellowship, so with the permission of my elders, it was agreed that I could start a Bible Study on Thursdays. My first Bible Study was at HMP Swaleside and now I was doing one at Elmcor. I would leave work, take the train home, and wait for the bus. Most evenings after work I was hungry because I did not have lunch money and had to settle for the free hot chocolate that was in the break room at Channel Thirteen. In the winter months when the bus took a long time, I would walk in the snow to get to Elmcor, hungry stomach and all. There were times my shoes would be full of snow, but I persevered because there was a cause and it was both noble and worthy. The class grew and eventually there was a graduation. The ministry continued long after I relocated to Jacksonville, FL. I consider it a part of my legacy in life.

CRY LOUD AND SPARE NOT

Besides the outreach at Elmcor, I attended and shared my testimony at street meetings with Sister Glendina Farrell and Rev. Donald Armand. One day an Evangelist by the name of Lula Ward invited me to do outreach with her and her trusted assistant Valerie at the infamous Rikers Island Prison. I was coming full circle. I had visited a friend who was at Rikers and years before I was sent there myself when the cop lied and said I pulled a knife on him. Now, I was going back with the Gospel, The Good News. I relished the opportunity to do prison outreach because I knew personally the power of the Gospel to transform lives. I knew from firsthand experience because it was in a prison that my life was transformed. The first time I attended the Rikers Island Outreach, the guard at the front would not allow me to enter because he said my name was not on the list. The Evangelist Lula did her best to convince him to allow me to go in with them, but he was adamant. The moment we thought I would not be able to enter for that visit, a captain walked up and inquired what was going on. The guard explained to him that my name was not on the list for the ministry visit and the captain looked at him and said, "Let him in." The guard tried to object, but the captain repeated his words, this time more sternly and with a more serious look. I never had any problems entering the facility for ministry after that. I don't believe in co-incidences, I believe in God-incidences. I believe God Almighty destined me to be in the prison that day to share my testimony and he had an angel in the form of the captain to walk up at the kairos, or seasonable moment. In Psalm 37:23 David wrote, "the steps of a good man is ordered by the LORD; and he delighteth in His way." The goodness David referred to is not simply the good deed a person does, the Hebrew word for "Good" as David used it in Psalm 37:23 is the word geber (pronounced gheh'-ber) which means—a *valiant* man or *warrior*, a man who is mighty. A valiant warrior who is mighty in the things of God. God ordered his steps because he is spiritually in tune with the purpose and plan of Yahweh. God delights in that man's way. In verse 24 David went on to say, "Though he fall, he shall not be utterly cast down: for the LORD upholdeth him with his Hand." I was bold in teaching and standing for the word of God in the English prison. I used my evenings to teach and fellowship with other inmates and the Lord Most High upheld me with his Hand. When the captain spoke up for me, I knew The Most High had used him to open the door for me to share with his other valiant warriors, mighty men who were not afraid to stand for Him in prison. It is not easy being a disciple of Christ behind prison walls. Many inmates convert to Islam because they get protection and in Islam it's an eye for an eye. I do understand some choose Islam because of the belief I once held about the white Jesus. A Christian soldier behind prison walls is a bonafide soldier. It had been the desire of my heart to be able to do prison ministry. My testimony was well-received by the brothers inside. At the end of one of the sessions, a muscular brother walked up to me and said, "The Lord said to tell you, 'Cry loud and spare not.'" It was a confirmation to me that God had raised me up from prison to be a mouthpiece for Him.

I do my best to honor the assignment with humility, realizing it is only the love, mercy, and grace of Abba which allows me to share His Word. From the life-changing destiny-impacting night that I bowed my head and my knees to the Lordship of Jesus Christ, I've endeavored to share the love of the Lord with great and small. My experience of eating the same oatmeal the pigs ate when I was at HMP Swaleside taught me not to look down on anyone no matter their lowly position in life. It is by the great mercy and grace of God that I was able to land on my feet after committing transgressions which could have ended my life, or at the very least sent me to prison for life.

I concur with a former prisoner who once wrote, "It is of the Lord's mercies that we are not consumed, because his compassions fail not. They are new every morning: great is thy faithfulness" (LAMENTATIONS 3:22-23 KJV). I committed the crime, so I refused to be bitter at the prospect of doing the time. As I studied the Bible, I realized many of the men used greatly by The Most High God spent time in prison or as in the case of Moses, were fugitives from justice. In Moses' case, he killed a man. I often think about Joseph and one of the many things written about him in the Bible, "And unto Joseph were born two sons before the years of famine came, which Asenath the daughter of Poti—phera priest of On bare unto him. And Joseph called the name of the firstborn Manasseh: For God, said he, hath made me forget all my toil, and all my father's house. And the name of the second called he Ephraim: For God hath caused me to be fruitful in the land of my affliction" (GENESIS 41:50-52 KJV). He could only be fruitful in the land of affliction when he was willing to forget all the negative toil he endured in his father's house. Sickness can cause a body to be afflicted with great pain and debilitation, a lengthy prison sentence can mean the land of affliction; a divorce, molestation, rape.

If you are going to make forward progress in terms of being fruitful, you must find a way to turn from the rearview mirror and look to the present and the future. You must not allow the pain of past failures, decisions which have you incarcerated, confined to a wheelchair or a hospital bed, to kill the inner creative seeds in you to facilitate fruit. Depression and despair will strangle the root and stop the production of fruit. Wherever you are, you are there for a purpose. Discover and fulfill your purpose and it will give you the freedom you so desire. Every time my cell door was shut and I heard the clicking sound, the jangling of the governor's keys, I reminded myself that I was in a place of separation for the purpose of preparation.

THE SCHOOL OF HARD KNOCKS

When I ministered at Elmcor, Rikers Island, and in street meetings, my goal was not to convince people to be Christians; my goal was to share the love of God manifested through Yashua the Savior which radically transformed my life. When people hear words like, Christian, church, the name Jesus Christ, all kinds of preconceived ideas and notions come to their mind. They tend to view those words through denominational lenses. I want them to know about the personal relationship I have with Jesus Christ, which did not come by way of denominationalism; it came through a life changing encounter at a very low point in my life. I want them to know that He wants them all to have the same transformation which comes through salvation. It is all about relationship and not religion. I didn't get to know Him in a comfortable building called a church after hearing a preacher preach his sermon. He manifested Himself in a place I call the school of hard knocks, a place I believe I was sent to in order to prepare me for my journey of divine freedom. Unlike the schools I attended when I was free, where I was not concerned about the grades I received, I purposed in my heart that I would graduate from the new school with honors. That school gave me the awareness of my true purpose in life and that purpose could not be fulfilled if I went back to my old life. It hardened my resolve never to be caged again for committing crimes. It prepared me mentally for the great things I vowed to do upon my release.

In October 2007, I was laid off along with many others from the real estate company where I worked. I knew the time was approaching where I would transition to full-time travel for ministry. In 2008, at the start of the Great Recession, my wife's cleaning business which was tied to the new home-building industry took a hit, so she and her niece closed the business. It had been a desire and a dream to do ministry full-time as a traveling evangelist. I would have to rely on God by faith just like I did in the English prison. The Lord told me when I was sent, I should not give my host an amount to give me because He would sustain me. He wanted to make sure I spoke the unadulterated word without sugar-coating it for monetary reasons. He kept me when I ate the oatmeal in HMP Swaleside that they fed the pigs, so I knew He could keep me and provide for me full-time. Over the years I travelled and ministered in places with small and large crowds—there are some churches where I go and don't take an offering at all because the ministry is struggling. My time in ministry, in prison, and walking and living by faith has prepared me for what I call such a time as this.

TRUST CHRIST IN THE CRISIS—
CORONA IS NOT KING

The crisis is a virus called Corona that is infecting and killing thousands of people. I've received calls and messages from childhood friends who have succumbed to the disease and died. It is global, affecting all nations; the effect for me is exacerbated by the fact that my wife and I lived by the gospel, and now our travel schedule is severely reduced. Movement is restricted as we are told to avoid public gatherings and practice social distancing. Many churches are not having meetings in their buildings, choosing instead to stream their services over social media. For the traveling evangelist it represents a major challenge, but God, I know Him to be Jehovah Jireh.

The coronavirus appears to be a plague of Biblical proportions. We were not created for social distancing by our Creator, we were created to have fellowship. For the sake of protecting life, we have to do something we were not created to do—stay away from one another. Inmates in prison have to be quarantined in their cells for most of the day and night. What effect will that have on their minds? It is like being in a prison within a prison. I found out earlier this morning that Gospel singer Troy Snead has died from contracting the virus. On the news yesterday, it was reported that a top E.R. Doctor named Lorna M. Breen, who worked at a Manhattan hospital hit hard by the coronavirus outbreak died by suicide. On the news they said she was overwhelmed by the things she saw as she did her job. Many hospital workers on the frontline treating patients and trying to save lives have died.

America, the wealthiest and most powerful country in the world, has become the epicenter of the virus. New York City, the city that never sleeps, the city Frank Sinatra sang about, has become the epicenter of the virus in America. People have lost millions of dollars on the stock market and in their retirement funds because of the volatility of the financial markets. This too shall pass, like many other viruses and plagues which preceded it, but many people are waking up to realize that no matter how sophisticated a nation is, no matter how wealthy, economically, and militarily powerful, they can wake up one day and face a crisis that is existential.

A crisis like this cannot be cured by the money they have in the bank; their nuclear and intercontinental ballistic missiles cannot protect them. Many are realizing they can be faced with a life-threatening crisis that the most brilliant scientific minds cannot solve. It lets mankind know it doesn't matter how lofty the heights he climbs. A microscopic virus, unseen by the naked eye, can turn the world in which he lives upside down. When examined under an electron microscope, the virus resembles a crown. "Corona" is the Latin word for crown and that is why they named it the coronavirus. The other name is COVID19. CO for Corona, VI or Virus, D for Disease and the 19 is for 2019, the year it surfaced in China. It is interesting to note that 19 is the Biblical number for faith and faith is tried by fire. This virus has definitely manifested to try the faith and trust on mankind. The jobs, businesses, and other entities people put their trust in are incapable of giving them peace of mind at the present time. The coronavirus is proving to be king of viruses in the way it has befuddled the nations.

When someone is about to be crowned king, a coronation is planned. In the word coronation you see the words corona and nation, meaning the one who wears the crown rules the nation. Over 2000 years ago, during the reign of a coronated king by the name of Herod, wise men travelled from the east to Jerusalem, saying, "Where is He that is born King of the Jews? For we have seen His star in the east and are come to worship Him" (MATTHEW 2:1-2). Though the men were wise they did not know the full council of The Most High, so they recognized that He was born king of the Jews but His full royal title would be—King of Kings and Lord of Lords. At the mention of His name, knees must bow and tongues must confess that Jesus Christ—Yashua ha Mesheach is Lord, to the glory of God Almighty. Every crisis gives an opportunity for the Sons of God not only to Present but to Re-Present the Christ. Megachurch buildings are shut because of restrictions on the number of people who can congregate in a building. Small and large churches have to use social media platforms like Facebook to get their message out. There is a new normal brought on by the virus that society has to adapt to, because no one knows when things will get back to the way they were. We must try to maintain a sense of normalcy in an abnormal time and season, while people are paranoid and fearful of being infected with this dreaded disease.

There is a shaking taking place across nations and only the spiritually fit and strong will survive. What shall it profit man or woman to gain the whole world and lose his or her soul? Or as Yashua went on to say, "Or what shall a man give in exchange for his soul?" (MARK 8:36-37) The soul is where a person's intellect, will, and emotions are housed. Someone can have all the riches possible, but if they lack the peace of mind that only The Prince Of Peace can give, they are poor and wretched. Prior to the outbreak of the coronavirus in America, the current administration was planning on cutting money allocated to free lunch programs which would affect children in poor communities. Low unemployment numbers were being touted and boasted about; Corona has caused millions of people to file for unemployment. Many of them have gone weeks, some months without getting an unemployment check. There was talk of actions being undertaken to deport people who were here illegally. In the news, we kept hearing about building a wall to keep people out. There was much division in the country when the coronavirus came. The lives of people all over the country were threatened physically, economically, and otherwise.

People are protesting in some cities to try to get governors to open their cities back up. Other people are protesting asking the government to get landlords and mortgage companies to waive payments until the crisis is under control. At one protest there were men who went into a state capital with high-powered weapons over their shoulders. If the crisis keeps up or if there is another wave of deaths which forces cities to shut down, there will be pandemonium in the streets. Trillions of dollars in stimulus money had to be released to help people and businesses and billions more will have to be released before all is said and done. No one is talking about cutting food stamps, free lunch, building walls, and deporting people right now. Corona is the boss for the time-being because everyone is talking about it. It is on every news cycle, I'm sure not one day has gone by since it started killing people that is has not been the lead story in the news, both cable and print. As I minister on radio, social media, and the rare times I am in front of a congregation, I tell people to be careful and not fearful—don't panic in the pandemic. I tell them that every crisis is an opportunity for something greater. In any crisis, there must not only be a plan to get through it but to prosper in and through it. Necessity is the mother of all inventions. The current crisis is coronavirus, but others will follow it. Matthew 24 records things Jesus said would befall the earth, in verse eight He described them as, "the beginning of sorrows." If this is what the beginning is like then there will be weeping and gnashing of teeth when a greater crisis hits, and it is only a matter of time before one does.

We are witnessing the global catastrophic impact one virus is causing, and it makes me wonder what life will be like when multiple tragedies hit the earth at the same time. Almost every year we hear of some virus like Ebola, bird flu, or H1N1. The last time I can remember when there was a virus which caused people around the world to be panic stricken was HIV—coronavirus is taking a greater toll because people looked at AIDS as a homosexual disease. The coronavirus is affecting all demographics. Like Michael Jackson said in his song, "it doesn't matter if you're black or white." The virus is killing black, white, and all other ethnic groups. It kills the educated and the uneducated. It kills male and female, young and old. People are in hospitals dying and in their last moments on earth they don't have family members at their bedside. People can't plan funerals the way they desire to because of the virus. I heard a nurse being interviewed on the radio today and she was asked what she did when someone is nearing the end. She said she held their hands and did her best to encourage them. Hopefully this will be a wake-up call to spread more love and kindness in the world rather than bigotry and hatred. It doesn't matter how superior someone thinks they are because of the color of their skin, educational level, or the wealth they have amassed. None of those things can stop the Grim Reaper when he pulls their number.

There is a certain balance and equilibrium to nature. Nature has laws and when they are violated through hatred, greed, or perversion, the people of the earth will have to deal with the consequences. We tend to be reactive and not proactive. Some people choose to live like God does not exist and when calamity strikes, they wonder why. 2020 represents the end of a decade. To me, this virus has set the tone for the close of the decade and has given the world a warning of things to come. Tenor Saw's song about "life being one big road with a lot of signs," is in my mind again. When the signposts of life are ignored—the effect will be occurrences which we cannot ignore. As governors, mayors, and others in authority give in to economic and social pressures and start opening things up for people to go back to work, go shopping, and do other things they took for granted before the crisis, will there be a second wave of deaths because the virus has not been contained? Only time will tell.

I pray for the diamonds in the rough who are still living the street life, the ones who are locked in a prison. Sharpening their minds through discipline and dedication, reading and studying; refusing to allow the negativity of their environments to breed animalistic tendencies. Instead, they work hard to be reformers, transformers in an often criminal in-justice system. They must make the most of a tragic situation by accepting a mission which many deem impossible, a mission to show society there is more to them than their prison-issued number, or what the rap sheet says. I pray for the advocates of social justice, tireless workers for a more just society. The kind of society Christ, King, X, Evers, and so many others gave their lives for. A society where the playing field is level, and everyone has the opportunity to be all they can be. A society free of racism, sexism, and all forms of isms and schisms. It is an uphill battle, because the reactionary minds of some conjure thoughts of a time of supremacy for some and subjugation for others. As Chuck D And Public Enemy said, "We must fight the powers that be." Junior Reid said, "Babylon release de chain but dem a use dem brains." He went on to say,

"Oh it's a shame now we feeling pain
Oh it's a shame I'm a feeling pain
My brother and my sister going down the drain
Brother and my sister going down the drain
The babylon release the chain but dem a use dem brain
I want to know
The babylon release the chain but dem a use dem brain"

Righteous, conscious teachers must use their brains to counteract the wicked Babylonian to suppress the rights of the people. I use the pen, the pulpit, radio station, and social media platforms to advocate for truth; spiritual truth, financial truth, political truth and all forms of truth which dispel myths and lies used to suppress the inalienable rights given human beings by their Creator.

I sincerely desire the effect of the transparency of this autobiographical exposé to be a resource tool that is used to interdict in the life of men and women, young and old, black, white, and other, causing them to avert the destructive path that led me to be a resident of Her Majesty's Prisons Wormwood Scrubbs, Brixton Prison, Belmarsh, and Swaleside for three out of the eight year sentence I was given. The numbers three and eight have Biblical prophetic significance in terms of my journey to the King's Prison for Divine Freedom. Three represents resurrection and Divine completeness, and eight represents a new beginning. The sentence I was given and the number of years I served, proves to me that I was Divinely resurrected, made a new creature in Christ to fulfill my assignment of advocacy.

Experiences and environments awakened me to the true reality, that I was in The King's Prison: a school of hard knocks, taking lessons to become an effective advocate for lost souls, the under privileged, the ones who feel there is no way out. If one soul averts the destruction that a life of perdition can cause, my time in The King's Prison—my Journey of Divine Freedom would be considered worthwhile.

Notes

1. *Foreign Relations of the United States, 1958–1960, Cuba, Volume VI - Office of the Historian*. https://history.state.gov/historicaldocuments/frus1958-60v06/d287. Accessed 27 May 2020.

2. "THE ANTI-SLAVERY SOCIETY; Exciting Debate and Final Action on Mr. Gurrison's Resolution of Dissolu-tion.The Society Votes to Live, by the Vote of 118 to 48. Mr. Garrison Retires from the Body and Mr.Phillips Suc-ceeds Him. Addresses of Anna E. Dickinson, Senator Wilson, William Lloyd Garrison, Frederick Douglass, Wendell Phillips, and Others. SECOND DAY'S SESSION. RESOLUTIONS SPEECH OF MR. SPAULDING. SPEECH OF MR. MAY. WHAT IS TO BE DONE? SPEECH OF MR. BOWDITCH. SPEECH OF FRED. DOUGLASS. SPEECH OF MR. FOSTER. A SPICY DEBATE. SPEECH OF ANNA DICKINSON. SHE DISLIKES SHERMAN. SHE DISAP-PROVES OF OTHER SOCIETIES. SPEECH OF SENATOR WILSON. SPEECH OF WM. L. GARRISON. SLAV-ERY IS DEAD. HIMSELF AND HIS FRIENDS. THE DAY OF JUBILEE. HE DECLINES. SPEECH OF WENDELL PHILLIPS. FINAL SCENES. THE RESULT." *The New York Times*, 11 May 1865. *NYTimes.com*, https://www.nytimes.com/1865/05/11/archives/the-antislavery-society-exciting-debate-and-final-action-on-mr.html.

3. *Queens College, City University of New York*. https://www.qc.cuny.edu/Academics/SupportPrograms/Seek/Pages/default.aspx. Accessed 27 May 2020.

4. Fried, Joseph P. "In Surprise, Witness Says Officer Bragged About Louima Torture." *The New York Times*, 20 May 1999. NYTimes.com, https://www.nytimes.com/1999/05/20/nyregion/in-surprise-witness-says-officer-bragged-about-louima-torture.html.

For
Speaking Engagements,
Book Signings,
Appearances,
and
Interviews...

CONTACT
Fidel Donaldson Ministries
3456 Turkey Oaks Dr. W.
Jacksonville, FL. 32277

904-881-1886
fidel_donaldson@yahoo.com

Made in the USA
Columbia, SC
18 June 2020